BEST-LOVED POEMS

BEST-LOVED POEMS

Edited by Neil Philip

Illustrated by Isabelle Brent

INDEX

For My Mother

A LITTLE, BROWN BOOK

First published in Great Britain in 2000
by Little, Brown and Company
First paperbacked in Great Britain in 2002
by Little, Brown

Reprinted 2003 (twice)

This edition published 2004 for Index Books Ltd

ISBN 0-316-72438-6

Printed and bound in Singapore

Little, Brown
An imprint of
Time Warner Books UK
Brettenham House
Lancaster Place
London WC2E 7EN

www.TimeWarnerBooks.co.uk

CONTENTS

OF CHILDHOOD AND YOUTH

OF LOVE AND MARRIAGE

OF LIFE

OF LOSS AND COMFORT

OF WAR AND PEACE

TO READ ALOUD

TO READ QUIETLY

OF ANIMALS AND NATURE

OF MAGIC AND MYSTERY

OF CHILDHOOD AND YOUTH

Infant Joy

I have no name.
I am but two days old.
What shall I call thee?
I happy am,
Joy is my name.
Sweet joy befall thee!

Pretty Joy!
Sweet Joy but two days old.
Sweet Joy I call thee!
Thou dost smile,
I sing the while.
Sweet joy befall thee!

William Blake

Pippa's Song

The year's at the spring,
And day's at the morn;
Morning's at seven;
The hill-side's dew-pearl'd;
The lark's on the wing;
The snail's on the thorn;
God's in His heaven—
All's right with the world!

Robert Browning

Children's Song

We live in our own world,
A world that is too small
For you to stoop and enter
Even on hands and knees,
The adult subterfuge.
And though you probe and pry
With analytic eye,
And eavesdrop all our talk
With an amused look,
You cannot find the centre
Where we dance, where we play,
Where life is still asleep
Under the closed flower,
Under the smooth shell
Of eggs in the cupped nest
That mock the faded blue
Of your remoter heaven.

R. S. Thomas

Wynken, Blynken, and Nod

Wynken, Blynken, and Nod one night
   Sailed off in a wooden shoe—
Sailed on a river of crystal light,
   Into a sea of dew.
"Where are you going, and what do you wish?"
   The old moon asked the three.
   "We have come to fish for the herring fish
   That live in this beautiful sea;
   Nets of silver and gold have we!"
     Said Wynken,
     Blynken,
     And Nod.

The old moon laughed and sang a song,
   As they rocked in the wooden shoe,
And the wind that sped them all night long
   Ruffled the waves of dew.
The little stars were the herring fish
   That lived in that beautiful sea—
   "Now cast your nets wherever you wish—
   Never afeard are we";
   So cried the stars to the fishermen three:
     Wynken,
     Blynken,
     And Nod.

All night long their nets they threw
   To the stars in the twinkling foam—
Then down from the skies came the wooden shoe,
   Bringing the fishermen home;
'Twas all so pretty a sail it seemed
   As if it could not be,
And some folks thought 'twas a dream they'd dreamed
   Of sailing that beautiful sea—
   But I shall name you the fishermen three:
      Wynken,
      Blynken,
      And Nod.

Wynken and Blynken are two little eyes,
   And Nod is a little head,
And the wooden shoe that sailed the skies
   Is the wee one's trundle-bed.
So shut your eyes while mother sings
   Of wonderful sights that be,
And you shall see the beautiful things
   As you rock in the misty sea,
   Where the old shoe rocked the fishermen three:
      Wynken,
      Blynken,
      And Nod.

Eugene Field

Apple Blossom

The first blossom was the best blossom
For the child who never had seen an orchard;
For the youth whom whisky had led astray
The morning after was the first day.

The first apple was the best apple
For Adam before he heard the sentence;
When the flaming sword endorsed the Fall
The trees were his to plant for all.

The first ocean was the best ocean
For the child from streets of doubt and litter;
For the youth for whom the skies unfurled
His first love was his first world.

But the first verdict seemed the worst verdict
When Adam and Eve were expelled from Eden;
Yet when the bitter gates clanged to
The sky beyond was just as blue.

For the next ocean is the first ocean
And the last ocean is the first ocean
And, however often the sun may rise,
A new thing dawns upon our eyes.

For the last blossom is the first blossom
And the first blossom is the best blossom
And when from Eden we take our way
The morning after is the first day.

Louis MacNeice

Advice to Young Children

"Children who paddle where the ocean bed shelves steeply
Must take great care they do not,
Paddle too deeply."

Thus spake the awful aging couple
Whose heart the years had turned to rubble.

But the little children, to save any bother,
Let it in at one ear and out at the other.

Stevie Smith

A Terrible Infant

I recollect a nurse called Ann,
    Who carried me about the grass,
And one fine day a fair young man
    Came up and kissed the pretty lass:
She did not make the least objection!
        Thinks I, *Aha!*
When I can talk I'll tell Mamma!
—And that's my earliest recollection.

Frederick Locker-Lampson

I Remember, I Remember

I remember, I remember,
The house where I was born,
The little window where the sun
Came peeping in at morn;
He never came a wink too soon,
Nor brought too long a day,
But now, I often wish the night
Had borne my breath away!

I remember, I remember,
The roses, red and white,
The violets, and the lily-cups,
Those flowers made of light!
The lilacs where the robin built,
And where my brother set
The laburnum on his birthday,—
The tree is living yet!

I remember, I remember,
Where I was used to swing,
And thought the air must rush as fresh
To swallows on the wing;
My spirit flew in feathers then,
That is so heavy now,
And summer pools could hardly cool
The fever on my brow!

I remember, I remember,
The fir trees dark and high;
I used to think their slender tops
Were close against the sky:
It was a childish ignorance,
But now 'tis little joy
To know I'm farther off from heaven
Than when I was a boy.

Thomas Hood

There Was a Little Girl

There was a little girl
Who had a little curl
Right in the middle of her forehead.
When she was good
She was very, very good,
But when she was bad she was horrid.

Henry Wadsworth Longfellow

To a Child

When I was a child I saw
a burning bird in a tree.
I see became *I am*,
I am became *I see.*

In winter dawns of frost
the lamp swung in my hand.
The battered moon on the slope
lay like a dune of sand,

And in the trap at my feet
the rabbit leapt and prayed,
weeping blood, and crouched
when the light shone on the blade.

The sudden sun lit up
the webs from wire to wire;
the white webs, the white dew,
blazed with a holy fire.

Flame of light in the dew,
flame of blood on the bush
answered the whirling sun
and the voice of the early thrush.

I think of this for you.
I would not have you believe
the world is empty of truth
or that men must grieve,

but hear the song of the martyrs
out of a bush of fire—
"All is consumed with love;
all is renewed with desire."

Judith Wright

The Unexplorer

There was a road ran past our house
Too lovely to explore.
I asked my mother once—she said
That if you followed where it led
It brought you to the milk-man's door.
(That's why I have not travelled more.)

Edna St. Vincent Millay

A Boy's Song

Where the pools are bright and deep,
Where the grey trout lies asleep,
Up the river and o'er the lea,
That's the way for Billy and me.

Where the blackbird sings the latest,
Where the hawthorn blooms the sweetest,
Where the nestlings chirp and flee,
That's the way for Billy and me.

Where the mowers mow the cleanest,
Where the hay lies thick and greenest;
There to trace the homeward bee,
That's the way for Billy and me.

Where the hazel bank is steepest,
Where the shadow falls the deepest,
Where the clustering nuts fall free,
That's the way for Billy and me.

Why the boys should drive away
Little sweet maidens from the play,
Or love to banter and fight so well,
That's the thing I never could tell.

But this I know, I love to play,
Through the meadow, among the hay;
Up the water and o'er the lea,
That's the way for Billy and me.

James Hogg

The Railway Children

When we climbed the slopes of the cutting
We were eye-level with the white cups
Of the telegraph poles and the sizzling wires.

Like lovely freehand they curved for miles
East and miles west beyond us, sagging
Under their burden of swallows.

We were small and thought we knew nothing
Worth knowing. We thought words travelled the wires
In the shiny pouches of raindrops,

Each one seeded full with the light
Of the sky, the gleam of the lines, and ourselves
So infinitesimally scaled

We could stream through the eye of a needle.

Seamus Heaney

The Toys

My little Son, who look'd from thoughtful eyes
And moved and spoke in quiet grown-up wise,
Having my law the seventh time disobey'd,
I struck him, and dismiss'd
With hard words and unkiss'd,
—His Mother, who was patient, being dead.
Then, fearing lest his grief should hinder sleep,
I visited his bed,
But found him slumbering deep,
With darken'd eyelids, and their lashes yet
From his late sobbing wet.
And I, with moan,
Kissing away his tears, left others of my own;
For, on a table drawn beside his head,
He had put, within his reach,
A box of counters and a red-vein'd stone,
A piece of glass abraded by the beach,

And six or seven shells,
A bottle with bluebells,
And two French copper coins, ranged there with careful art,
To comfort his sad heart.
So when that night I pray'd
To God, I wept, and said:
Ah, when at last we lie with trancèd breath,
Not vexing Thee in death,
And Thou rememberest of what toys
We made our joys,
How weakly understood
Thy great commanded good,
Then, fatherly not less
Than I whom Thou hast moulded from the clay,
Thou'lt leave Thy wrath, and say,
"I will be sorry for their childishness."

Coventry Patmore

"Into my heart an air that kills"

Into my heart an air that kills
    From yon far country blows:
What are those blue remembered hills,
    What spires, what farms are those?

That is the land of lost content,
    I see it shining plain,
The happy highways where I went
    And cannot come again.

A. E. Housman

"The Angel that presided o'er my birth"

The Angel that presided o'er my birth
Said, "Little creature, formed of joy and mirth,
Go love without the help of any thing on earth."

William Blake

OF LOVE AND MARRIAGE

Girl, Boy, Flower, Bicycle

This girl
Waits at the corner for
This boy
Freewheeling on his bicycle.
She holds
A flower in her hand
A gold flower
In her hands she holds
The sun.
With power between his thighs
The boy
Comes smiling to her
He rides
A bicycle that glitters like
The wind.
This boy this girl
They walk
In step with the wind
Arm in arm
They climb the level street
To where
Laid on the glittering handlebars
The flower
Is round and shining as
The sun.

M. K. Joseph

Wild Nights

Wild nights! Wild nights!
Were I with thee,
Wild nights should be
Our luxury!

Futile the winds
To a heart in port,—
Done with the compass,
Done with the chart.

Rowing in Eden!
Ah! the sea!
Might I but moor
Tonight in thee!

Emily Dickinson

To His Coy Mistress

Had we but world enough, and time,
This coyness, Lady, were no crime.
We would sit down and think which way
To walk and pass our long love's day.
Thou by the Indian Ganges' side
Shouldst rubies find: I by the tide
Of Humber would complain. I would
Love you ten years before the Flood,
And you should, if you please, refuse
Till the conversion of the Jews.
My vegetable love should grow
Vaster than empires, and more slow;
An hundred years should go to praise
Thine eyes and on thy forehead gaze;
Two hundred to adore each breast;
But thirty thousand to the rest;
An age at least to every part,
And the last age should show your heart;
For, Lady, you deserve this state,
Nor would I love at lower rate.

But at my back I always hear
Time's wingèd chariot hurrying near;
And yonder all before us lie
Deserts of vast eternity.
Thy beauty shall no more be found,
Nor, in thy marble vault, shall sound
My echoing song: then worms shall try
That long preserved virginity,
And your quaint honour turn to dust,
And into ashes all my lust:
The grave's a fine and private place,
But none, I think, do there embrace.

Now therefore, while the youthful hue
Sits on thy skin like morning dew,
And while thy willing soul transpires
At every pore with instant fires,
Now let us sport us while we may,
And now, like amorous birds of prey,
Rather at once our time devour
Than languish in his slow-chapt power.
Let us roll all our strength and all
Our sweetness up into one ball,
And tear our pleasures with rough strife
Thorough the iron gates of life:
Thus, though we cannot make our sun
Stand still, yet we will make him run.

Andrew Marvell

Love and Life

All my past life is mine no more;
   The flying hours are gone,
Like transitory dreams given o'er
Whose images are kept in store
   By memory alone.

Whatever is to come is not:
   How can it then be mine?
The present moment's all my lot,
And that, as fast as it is got,
   Phyllis, is wholly thine.

Then talk not of inconstancy,
   False hearts, and broken vows;
If I, by miracle, can be
This livelong minute true to thee,
   'Tis all that heaven allows.

John Wilmot, Earl of Rochester

Love Is Enough

Love is enough: though the World be a-waning,
And the woods have no voice but the voice of complaining,
 Though the sky be too dark for dim eyes to discover
The gold-cups and daisies fair blooming thereunder,
Though the hills be held shadows, and the sea a dark wonder,
 And this day draw a veil over all deeds pass'd over,
Yet their hands shall not tremble, their feet shall not falter;
The void shall not weary, the fear shall not alter
 These lips and these eyes of the loved and the lover.

William Morris

Meeting at Night

The gray sea and the long black land;
And the yellow half-moon large and low;
And the startled little waves that leap
In fiery ringlets from their sleep,
As I gain the cove with pushing prow,
And quench its speed i'the slushy sand.

Then a mile of warm sea-scented beach;
Three fields to cross till a farm appears;
A tap at the pane, the quick sharp scratch
And blue spurt of a lighted match,
And a voice less loud, through its joys and fears,
Than the two hearts beating each to each!

Parting at Morning

Round the cape of a sudden came the sea,
And the sun looked over the mountain's rim:
And straight was a path of gold for him,
And the need of a world of men for me.

Robert Browning

Sonnet: "How do I love thee?"

How do I love thee? Let me count the ways.
I love thee to the depth and breadth and height
My soul can reach, when feeling out of sight
For the ends of Being and ideal Grace.
I love thee to the level of every day's
Most quiet need, by sun and candlelight.
I love thee freely, as men strive for Right;
I love thee purely, as they turn from Praise.
I love thee with the passion put to use
In my old griefs, and with my childhood's faith.
I love thee with a love I seemed to lose
With my lost saints,—I love thee with the breath,
Smiles, tears, of all my life!—and, if God choose,
I shall but love thee better after death.

Elizabeth Barrett Browning

A Red, Red Rose

My love is like a red, red rose
 That's newly sprung in June:
My love is like the melody
 That's sweetly played in tune.

As fair art thou, my bonnie lass,
 So deep in love am I:
And I will love thee still, my dear,
 Till a' the seas gang dry.

Till a' the seas gang dry, my dear,
 And the rocks melt wi' the sun:
And I will love thee still, my dear,
 While the sands o' life shall run.

And fare thee weel, my only love,
 And fare thee weel a while!
And I will come again, my love,
 Thou' it were ten thousand mile.

Robert Burns

He Wishes for the Cloths of Heaven

Had I the heavens' embroidered cloths,
Enwrought with golden and silver light,
The blue and the dim and the dark cloths
Of night and light and the half-light,
I would spread the cloths under your feet:
But I, being poor, have only my dreams;
I have spread my dreams under your feet;
Tread softly because you tread on my dreams.

W. B. Yeats

"She tells her love while half asleep"

She tells her love while half asleep
 In the dark hours,
  With half-words whispered low:
As Earth stirs in her winter sleep
 And puts out grass and flowers
  Despite the snow,
  Despite the falling snow.

Robert Graves

"i like my body when it is with your body"

i like my body when it is with your
body.   It is so quite new a thing.
Muscles better and nerves more.
i like your body.   i like what it does,
i like its hows.   i like to feel the spine
of your body and its bones,and the trembling
-firm-smooth ness and which i will
again and again and again
kiss,   i like kissing this and that of you,
i like,slowly stroking the,shocking fuzz
of your electric fur,and what-is-it comes
over parting flesh. . . . And eyes big love-crumbs,

and possibly i like the thrill

of under me you so quite new

E. E. Cummings

Western Wind

Western wind, when will thou blow,
  The small rain down can rain?
Christ, if my love were in my arms
  And I in my bed again!

Anon.

Victoria Market

I said to my companion, this is walking
I said to my companion, how my heart goes
   out to all lovers.

The darkness was still warm
but the fields were freshening beautifully
   in the winter rain;
the market was full of little lights
and I remarked the ear of a sack
sleeping on top of a tyre like a cat
   on the kerbstone

I said to my friend stop falling on your knees
I have to keep pulling you on to your feet again—
   then the dawn came down silently between
   the rows of vegetables
and we passed out into the white star
rejoicing companionless in our love

As I crossed the square on my way home
the highest spires were ablaze with the movement of feet.

Francis Brabazon

from **The Rubaiyat of Omar Khayyam**

A book of Verses underneath the Bough,
A Jug of Wine, a Loaf of Bread—and Thou
  Beside me singing in the Wilderness—
O, Wilderness were Paradise enow!

Edward Fitzgerald

Rondeau: "Jenny kissed me"

Jenny kissed me when we met,
  Jumping from the chair she sat in;
Time, you thief, who love to get
  Sweets into your list, put that in!
Say I'm weary, say I'm sad,
  Say that health and wealth have missed me,
Say I'm growing old, but add,
  Jenny kissed me.

Leigh Hunt

Reflection on Ice-breaking

Candy
Is dandy
But liquor
Is quicker.

Ogden Nash

Celia Celia

When I am sad and weary,
When I think all hope has gone,
When I walk along High Holborn
I think of you with nothing on.

Adrian Mitchell

"When a Man has Married a Wife"

When a Man has Married a Wife
    He finds out whether
Her Knees & Elbows are only
    Glued together.

William Blake

"She walks in beauty, like the night"

She walks in beauty, like the night
    Of cloudless climes and starry skies;
And all that's best of dark and bright
    Meet in her aspect and her eyes:
Thus mellowed to that tender light
    Which heaven to gaudy day denies.

One shade the more, one ray the less,
    Had half impaired the nameless grace
Which waves in every raven tress,
    Or softly lightens o'er her face;
Where thoughts serenely sweet express
    How pure, how dear their dwelling-place.

And on that cheek, and o'er that brow,
    So soft, so calm, yet eloquent,
The smiles that win, the tints that glow,
    But tell of days in goodness spent,
A mind at peace with all below,
    A heart whose love is innocent.

George Gordon Noel, Lord Byron

On Raglan Road

(Air: *The Dawning of The Day*)

On Raglan Road on an autumn day I met her first and knew
That her dark hair would weave a snare that I might
    one day rue;
I saw the danger, yet I walked along the enchanted way,
And I said, let grief be a fallen leaf at the dawning of the day.

On Grafton Street in November we tripped lightly
    along the ledge
Of the deep ravine where can be seen the worth
    of passion's pledge,
The Queen of Hearts still making tarts and I not
    making hay—
O I loved too much and by such by such is happiness
    thrown away.

I gave her gifts of the mind I gave her the secret sign
    that's known
To the artists who have known the true gods
    of sound and stone
And word and tint. I did not stint for I gave her
    poems to say.
With her own name there and her own dark hair like clouds
    over fields of May.

On a quiet street where old ghosts meet I see her
    walking now
Away from me so hurriedly my reason must allow
That I had wooed not as I should a creature made of clay—
When the angel woos the clay he'd lose his wings at the
    dawn of day.

Patrick Kavanagh

"O wert thou in the cauld blast"

O wert thou in the cauld blast,
　　On yonder lea, on yonder lea,
My plaidie to the angry airt,
　　I'd shelter thee, I'd shelter thee.
Or did misfortune's bitter storms
　　Around thee blaw, around thee blaw,
Thy bield should be my bosom,
　　To share it a', to share it a'.

Or were I in the wildest waste,
　　Sae black and bare, sae black and bare,
The desert were a Paradise,
　　If thou wert there, if thou wert there.
Or were I monarch o' the globe,
　　Wi' thee to reign, wi' thee to reign,
The brightest jewel in my crown
　　Wad be my queen, wad be my queen.

Robert Burns

What Ails Thee?

What ails thee then, woman, what ails thee?
doesn't ter know?
If tha canna say't, come then an' scraight it out on my bosom!
Eh?—Men doesna ha'e bosoms? 'appen not, on'y tha knows
    what I mean.
Come then, tha can scraight it out on my shirt-front
an' tha'lt feel better.

   —In the first place, I don't scraight.
   And if I did, I certainly couldn't *scraight it out.*
   And if I could, the last place I should choose
   would be your shirt-front
   or your manly bosom either.
   So leave off trying to put the Robbie Burns touch over me
   and kindly hand me the cigarettes
   if you haven't smoked them all,
   which you're much more likely to do
   than to shelter anybody from the cau-auld blast.—

D. H. Lawrence

49

Sonnet: "Let me not to the marriage of true minds"

Let me not to the marriage of true minds
    Admit impediments. Love is not love
Which alters when it alteration finds,
    Or bends with the remover to remove.
O, no! it is an ever-fixèd mark,
    That looks on tempests and is never shaken;
It is the star to every wandering bark,
    Whose worth's unknown, although his height be taken.
Love's not Time's fool, though rosy lips and cheeks
    Within his bending sickle's compass come;
Love alters not with his brief hours and weeks,
    But bears it out even to the edge of doom.
      If this be error, and upon me proved,
      I never writ, nor no man ever loved.

William Shakespeare

50

A Slice of Wedding Cake

Why have such scores of lovely, gifted girls
    Married impossible men?
Simple self-sacrifice may be ruled out,
    And missionary endeavour, nine times out of ten.

Repeat "impossible men": not merely rustic,
    Foul-tempered or depraved
(Dramatic foils chosen to show the world
    How well women behave, and always have behaved).

Impossible men: idle, illiterate,
    Self-pitying, dirty, sly,
For whose appearance even in City parks
    Excuses must be made to casual passers-by.

Has God's supply of tolerable husbands
    Fallen, in fact, so low?
Or do I always over-value woman
    At the expense of man?
                Do I?
                      It might be so.

Robert Graves

To Fanny Brawne

This living hand, now warm and capable
Of earnest grasping, would, if it were cold
And in the icy silence of the tomb,
So haunt thy days and chill thy dreaming nights
That thou wouldst wish thine own heart dry of blood
So in my veins red life might stream again,
And thou be conscience-calmed—see here it is—
I hold it towards you.

John Keats

His Late Wife's Wedding-Ring

The ring so worn, as you behold,
So thin, so pale, is yet of gold:
The passion such it was to prove;
Worn with life's cares, love yet was love.

George Crabbe

OF LIFE

Life is Fine

I went down to the river,
I set down on the bank.
I tried to think but couldn't,
So I jumped in and sank.

I came up once and hollered!
I came up twice and cried!
If that water hadn't a-been so cold
I might've sunk and died.

But it was
Cold in that water!
It was cold!

I took the elevator
Sixteen floors above the ground.
I thought about my baby
And thought I would jump down.

I stood there and I hollered!
I stood there and I cried!
If it hadn't a-been so high
I might've jumped and died.

But it was
High up there!
It was high!

So since I'm still here livin',
I guess I will live on.
I could've died for love—
But for livin' I was born.

Though you may hear me holler,
And you may see me cry—
I'll be dogged, sweet baby,
If you gonna see me die.

Life is fine!
Fine as wine!
Life is fine!

Langston Hughes

Wishes of an Elderly Man

I wish I loved the Human Race;
I wish I loved its silly face;
I wish I liked the way it walks;
I wish I liked the way it talks;
And when I'm introduced to one
I wish I thought *What Jolly Fun!*

Walter Raleigh

A Birthday

My heart is like a singing bird
   Whose nest is in a watered shoot;
My heart is like an apple-tree
   Whose boughs are bent with thickset fruit;
My heart is like a rainbow shell
   That paddles in a halcyon sea;
My heart is gladder than all these
   Because my love is come to me.

Raise me a dais of silk and down;
   Hang it with vair and purple dyes;
Carve it in doves and pomegranates,
   And peacocks with a hundred eyes;
Work it in gold and silver grapes,
   In leaves and silver fleurs-de-lys;
Because the birthday of my life
   Is come, my love is come to me.

Christina Rossetti

Self-Pity

I never saw a wild thing
sorry for itself.
A small bird will drop frozen dead from a bough
without ever having felt sorry for itself.

D. H. Lawrence

"The master, the swabber, the boatswain and I"

The master, the swabber, the boatswain and I,
   The gunner and his mate,
Loved Mall, Meg, and Marian, and Margery,
   But none of us cared for Kate.
   For she had a tongue with a tang,
   Would cry to a sailor, "Go hang!"
She loved not the savour of tar nor of pitch,
Yet a tailor might scratch her where'er she did itch.
   Then to sea, boys, and let her go hang.

William Shakespeare

Bad Women

Oh the gladness of a woman when she's glad!
And oh the sadness of a woman when she's sad!
      But the gladness of her gladness
      And the sadness of her sadness
Are nothing to her badness when she's bad!

Anon.

How Pleasant It Is to Have Money

As I sat at the café, I said to myself,
They may talk as they please about what they call pelf,
They may sneer as they like about eating and drinking,
But help it I cannot, I cannot help thinking,
    How pleasant it is to have money, heigh ho!
    How pleasant it is to have money.

I sit at my table *en grand seigneur,*
And when I have done, throw a crust to the poor;
Not only the pleasure, one's self, of good living,
But also the pleasure of now and then giving.
    So pleasant it is to have money, heigh ho!
    So pleasant it is to have money.

It was but last winter I came up to Town,
But already I'm getting a little renown;
I make new acquaintance where'er I appear
I am not too shy, and have nothing to fear.
    So pleasant it is to have money, heigh ho!
    So pleasant it is to have money.

I drive through the streets, and I care not a damn;
The people they stare, and they ask who I am;
And if I should chance to run over a cad,
I can pay for the damage if ever so bad.
    So pleasant it is to have money, heigh ho!
    So pleasant it is to have money.

We stroll to our box and look down on the pit,
And if it weren't low should be tempted to spit;
We loll and we talk until people look up,
And when it's half over we go out and sup.
  So pleasant it is to have money, heigh ho!
  So pleasant it is to have money.

The best of the tables and best of the fare—
And as for the others, the devil may care;
It isn't our fault if they dare not afford
To sup like a prince and be drunk as a lord.
  So pleasant it is to have money, heigh ho!
  So pleasant it is to have money.

We sit at our tables and tipple champagne;
Ere one bottle goes, comes another again;
The waiters they skip and they scuttle about,
And the landlord attends us so civilly out.
  So pleasant it is to have money, heigh ho!
  So pleasant it is to have money.

It was but last winter I came up to town,
But already I'm getting a little renown;
I get to good houses without much ado,
Am beginning to see the nobility too.
  So pleasant it is to have money, heigh ho!
  So pleasant it is to have money.

O dear! what a pity they ever should lose it!
For they are the gentry that know how to use it;
So grand and so graceful, such manners, such dinners,
But yet, after all, it is we are the winners.
  So pleasant it is to have money, heigh ho!
  So pleasant it is to have money.

Thus I sat at my table *en grand seigneur,*
And when I had done threw a crust to the poor;
Not only the pleasure, one's self, of good eating,
But also the pleasure of now and then treating.
   So pleasant it is to have money, heigh ho!
   So pleasant it is to have money.

They may talk as they please about what they call pelf,
And how one ought never to think of one's self,
And how pleasures of thought surpass eating and drinking—
My pleasure of thought is the pleasure of thinking
   How pleasant it is to have money, heigh ho!
   How pleasant it is to have money.

A gondola here, and a gondola there,
'Tis the pleasantest fashion of taking the air.
To right and to left; stop, turn, and go yonder,
And let us repeat, o'er the tide as we wander,
   How pleasant it is to have money, heigh ho!
   How pleasant it is to have money.

Arthur Hugh Clough

Riches

When I wish I was rich, then I know I am ill.
Because, to tell the truth, I have enough as I am.
So when I catch myself thinking: Ah, if I was rich—!
I say to myself: Hello! I'm not well. My vitality is low.

D. H. Lawrence

"Oh dear! How disgusting is life!"

O dear! How disgusting is life!
To improve it O what can we do?
Most disgusting is hustle and strife,
and of all things an ill-fitting shoe—
shoe,
O bother an ill-fitting shoe!

Edward Lear

The Embankment

(The fantasia of a fallen gentleman on a cold, bitter night)

Once, in finesse of fiddles found I ecstasy,
In a flash of gold heels on the hard pavement.
Now see I
That warmth's the very stuff of poesy.
Oh, God, make small
The old star-eaten blanket of the sky,
That I may fold it round me and in comfort lie.

T. E. Hulme

The Skip

I took my life and threw it on the skip,
Reckoning the next-door neighbours wouldn't mind
If my life hitched a lift to the council tip
With their dry rot and rubble. What you find

With skips is—the whole community joins in.
Old mattresses appear, doors kind of drift
Along with all that won't fit in the bin
And what the bin-men can't be fished to shift.

I threw away my life, and there it lay
And grew quite sodden. "What a dreadful shame,"
Clucked some old bag and sucked her teeth: "The way
The young these days . . . no values . . . me, I blame . . ."

But I blamed no one. Quality control
Had loused it up, and that was that. 'Nough said.
I couldn't stick at home. I took a stroll
And passed the skip, and left my life for dead.

Without my life, the beer was just as foul,
The landlord still as filthy as his wife,
The chicken in the basket was an owl,
And no one said: "Ee, Jim-lad, whur's thee life?"

Well, I got back that night the worse for wear,
But still just capable of single vision;
Looked in the skip; my life—it wasn't there!
Some bugger'd nicked it—*without* my permission.

Okay, so I got angry and began
To shout, and woke the street. Okay. *Okay!*
And I was sick all down the neighbour's van.
And I disgraced myself on the par-*kay*.

And then . . . you know how if you've had a few
You'll wake at dawn, all healthy, like sea breezes,
Raring to go, and thinking: "Clever you!
You've got away with it." And then, oh Jesus,

It hits you. Well, that morning, just at six
I woke, got up and looked down at the skip.
There lay my life, still sodden, on the bricks;
There lay my poor old life, arse over tip.

Or was it mine? Still dressed, I went downstairs
And took a long cool look. The truth was dawning.
Someone had just exchanged my life for theirs.
Poor fool, I thought—I should have left a warning.

Some bastard saw my life and thought it nicer
Than what he had. Yet what he'd had seemed fine.
He'd never caught his fingers in the slicer
The way I'd managed in that life of mine.

His life lay glistening in the rain, neglected,
Yet still a decent, an authentic life.
Some people I can think of, I reflected
Would take that thing as soon as you'd say Knife.

It seemed a shame to miss a chance like that.
I brought the life in, dried it by the stove.
It looked so fetching, stretched out on the mat.
I tried it on. It fitted, like a glove.

And now, when some local bat drops off the twig
And new folk take the house, and pull up floors
And knock down walls and hire some kind of big
Container (say, a skip) for their old doors,

I'll watch it like a hawk, and every day
I'll make at least—oh—half a dozen trips.
I've furnished an existence in that way.
You'd not believe the things you find on skips.

James Fenton

64

Heredity

I am the family face;
Flesh perishes, I live on,
Projecting trait and trace
Through time to times anon,
And leaping from place to place
Over oblivion.

The years-heired feature that can
In curve and voice and eye
Despise the human span
Of durance—that is I;
The eternal thing in man,
That heeds no call to die.

Thomas Hardy

Days

What are days for?
Days are where we live.
They come, they wake us
Time and time over.
They are to be happy in:
Where can we live but days?

Ah, solving that question
Brings the priest and the doctor
In their long coats
Running over the fields.

Philip Larkin

Letters

Every day brings a ship,
Every ship brings a word;
Well for those who have no fear,
Looking seaward, well assured
That the word the vessel brings
Is the word they wish to hear.

Ralph Waldo Emerson

This Be The Verse

They fuck you up, your mum and dad.
   They may not mean to, but they do.
They fill you with the faults they had
   And add some extra, just for you.

But they were fucked up in their turn
   By fools in old-style hats and coats,
Who half the time were soppy-stern
   And half at one another's throats.

Man hands on misery to man.
   It deepens like a coastal shelf.
Get out as early as you can,
   And don't have any kids yourself.

Philip Larkin

My Own Epitaph

Life is a jest; and all things show it,
I thought so once; but now I know it.

John Gay

The Magpies

When Tom and Elizabeth took the farm
The bracken made their bed,
And *Quardle oodle ardle wardle doodle*
The magpies said.

Tom's hand was strong to the plough
Elizabeth's lips were red,
And *Quardle oodle ardle wardle doodle*
The magpies said.

Year in year out they worked
While the pines grew overhead,
And *Quardle oodle ardle wardle doodle*
The magpies said.

But all the beautiful crops soon went
To the mortgage-man instead,
And *Quardle oodle ardle wardle doodle*
The magpies said.

Elizabeth is dead now (it's years ago);
Old Tom went light in the head;
And *Quardle oodle ardle wardle doodle*
The magpies said.

The farm's still there. Mortgage corporations
Couldn't give it away.
And *Quardle oodle ardle wardle doodle*
The magpies say.

Denis Glover

Richard Cory

Whenever Richard Cory went down town,
We people on the pavement looked at him:
He was a gentleman from sole to crown,
Clean favored, and imperially slim.

And he was always quietly arrayed,
And he was always human when he talked;
But still he fluttered pulses when he said,
"Good-morning," and he glittered when he walked.

And he was rich—yes, richer than a king—
And admirably schooled in every grace:
In fine, we thought that he was everything
To make us wish that we were in his place.

So on we worked, and waited for the light,
And went without the meat, and cursed the bread;
And Richard Cory, one calm summer night,
Went home and put a bullet through his head.

Edwin Arlington Robinson

Mr. Jones

"There's been an accident!" they said,
"Your servant's cut in half; he's dead!"
"Indeed!" said Mr Jones, "and please
Send me the half that's got my keys."

Harry Graham

"In the desert"

In the desert
I saw a creature, naked, bestial,
Who, squatting upon the ground,
Held his heart in his hands,
And ate of it.
I said, "Is it good, friend?"
"It is bitter—bitter," he answered;
"But I like it
Because it is bitter,
And because it is my heart."

Stephen Crane

The False Heart

I said to Heart, "How goes it?" Heart replied:
"Right as a Ribstone Pippin!" But it lied.

Hilaire Belloc

This Is Just to Say

I have eaten
the plums
that were in
the icebox

and which
you were probably
saving
for breakfast

Forgive me
they were delicious
so sweet
and so cold

William Carlos Williams

Delight in Disorder

A sweet disorder in the dress
Kindles in clothes a wantonness:
A lawn about the shoulders thrown
Into a fine distraction:
An erring lace, which here and there
Enthrals the crimson stomacher:
A cuff neglectful, and thereby
Ribbands to flow confusedly:
A winning wave, deserving note,
In the tempestuous petticoat:
A careless shoe-string, in whose tie
I see a wild civility:
Do more bewitch me than when art
Is too precise in every part.

Robert Herrick

The Oak

Live thy Life,
   Young and old,
Like yon oak,
Bright in spring,
   Living gold;

Summer-rich
   Then; and then
Autumn-changed,
Soberer-hued
   Gold again.

All his leaves
   Fall'n at length,
Look, he stands,
Trunk and bough,
   Naked strengh.

Alfred, Lord Tennyson

Desire Is Dead

Desire may be dead
and still a man can be
a meeting place for sun and rain,
wonder outwaiting pain
as in a wintry tree.

D. H. Lawrence

Remembrance

They flee from me, that sometime did me seek
   With naked foot, stalking in my chamber.
I have seen them gentle, tame, and meek,
   That now are wild, and do not remember
   That sometime they put themselves in danger
      To take bread at my hand; and now they range
      Busily seeking with a continual change.

Thanked be fortune it hath been otherwise
   Twenty times better; but once, in special,
In thin array, after a pleasant guise,
   When her loose gown from her shoulders did fall,
   And she me caught in her arms long and small,
      Therewith all sweetly did me kiss
      And softly said, "Dear heart, how like you this?"

It was no dream; I lay broad waking:
   But all is turned, thorough my gentleness,
Into a strange fashion of forsaking;
   And I have leave to go of her goodness,
   And she also to use newfangleness.
      But since that I so kindly am served,
      I would fain know what she hath deserved.

Sir Thomas Wyatt

Sea-Fever

I must go down to the seas again, to the lonely sea
    and the sky,
And all I ask is a tall ship and a star to steer her by,
And the wheel's kick and the wind's song and the white
    sails shaking,
And a grey mist on the sea's face and a grey dawn breaking.

I must go down to the seas again, for the call of the
    running tide
Is a wild call and a clear call that may not be denied;
And all I ask is a windy day with the white clouds flying,
And the flung spray and the blown spume, and the
    sea-gulls crying.

I must go down to the seas again, to the vagrant gypsy life,
To the gull's way and the whale's way where the wind's
    like a whetted knife;
And all I ask is a merry yarn from a laughing fellow-rover,
And quiet sleep and a sweet dream when the long
    trick's over.

John Masefield

Sound, Sound the Clarion

Sound, sound the clarion, fill the fife!
  Throughout the sensual world proclaim,
One crowded hour of glorious life
  Is worth an age without a name.

Thomas Osbert Mordaunt

First Fig

My candle burns at both ends;
  It will not last the night;
But ah, my foes, and oh, my friends!—
  It gives a lovely light!

Edna St. Vincent Millay

OF LOSS AND COMFORT

"Life is mostly froth and bubble"

Life is mostly froth and bubble,
Two things stand like stone,
Kindness in another's trouble,
Courage in your own.

Adam Lindsay Gordon

"In this short Life"

In this short Life
That only lasts an hour
How much—how little—is
Within our power

Emily Dickinson

On His Seventy-Fifth Birthday

I strove with none, for none was worth my strife.
Nature I loved and, next to Nature, Art:
I warmed both hands before the fire of Life;
It sinks, and I am ready to depart.

Walter Savage Landor

Invictus

Out of the night that covers me,
    Black as the Pit from pole to pole,
I thank whatever gods may be
    For my unconquerable soul.

In the fell clutch of circumstance
    I have not winced nor cried aloud.
Under the bludgeonings of chance
    My head is bloody, but unbowed.

Beyond this place of wrath and tears
    Looms but the Horror of the shade,
And yet the menace of the years
    Finds, and shall find, me unafraid.

It matters not how strait the gate,
    How charged with punishments the scroll,
I am the master of my fate:
    I am the captain of my soul.

W. E. Henley

Last Lines

"The following are the last lines my sister Emily ever wrote."
(*Charlotte Brontë*)

No coward soul is mine,
No trembler in the world's storm-troubled sphere:
I see Heaven's glories shine,
And faith shines equal, arming me from fear.

O God within my breast,
Almighty, ever-present Deity!
Life—that in me has rest,
As I—undying Life—have power in thee!

Vain are the thousand creeds
That move men's hearts: unutterably vain;
Worthless as withered weeds,
Or idlest froth amid the boundless main,

To waken doubt in one
Holding so fast by thine infinity;
So surely anchored on
The steadfast rock of immortality.

With wide-embracing love
Thy spirit animates eternal years,
Pervades and broods above,
Changes, sustains, dissolves, creates, and rears.

Though earth and man were gone,
And suns and universes ceased to be,
And thou were left alone,
Every existence would exist in thee.

There is not room for Death,
Nor atom that his might could render void:
Thou—thou art Being and Breath,
And what thou art may never be destroyed.

Emily Brontë

I Am

I am: yet what I am none cares or knows,
　My friends forsake me like a memory lost;
I am the self-consumer of my woes,
　They rise and vanish in oblivious host,
Like shades in love and death's oblivion lost;
And yet I am, and live with shadows tost

Into the nothingness of scorn and noise,
　Into the living sea of waking dreams,
Where there is neither sense of life nor joys,
　But the vast shipwreck of my life's esteems;
And e'en the dearest—that I loved the best—
Are strange—nay, rather stranger than the rest.

I long for scenes where man has never trod,
　A place where woman never smiled or wept;
There to abide with my Creator, God,
　And sleep as I in childhood sweetly slept:
Untroubling and untroubled where I lie,
The grass below—above the vaulted sky.

John Clare

The Woodspurge

The wind flapped loose, the wind was still,
Shaken out dead from tree and hill:
I had walked on at the wind's will,—
I sat now, for the wind was still.

Between my knees my forehead was,—
My lips, drawn in, said not Alas!
My hair was over in the grass,
My naked ears heard the day pass.

My eyes, wide open, had the run
Of some ten weeds to fix upon;
Among those few, out of the sun,
The woodspurge flowered, three cups in one.

From perfect grief there need not be
Wisdom or even memory:
One thing then learnt remains to me,—
The woodspurge has a cup of three.

Dante Gabriel Rossetti

The Walk

You did not walk with me
Of late to the hill-top tree
  By the gated ways,
  As in earlier days;
  You were weak and lame,
  So you never came,
And I went alone, and I did not mind,
Not thinking of you as left behind.

I walked up there to-day
Just in the former way;
  Surveyed around
  The familiar ground
  By myself again:
  What difference, then?
Only that underlying sense
Of the look of a room on returning thence.

Thomas Hardy

A Lament

O world! O life! O time!
On whose last steps I climb,
   Trembling at that where I had stood before;
When will return the glory of your prime?
      No more—Oh, never more!

Out of the day and night
A joy has taken flight;
   Fresh spring, and summer, and winter hoar,
Move my faint heart with grief, but with delight
      No more—Oh, never more!

Percy Bysshe Shelley

Epitaph

Even such is Time, which takes in trust
Our youth, our joys, and all we have,
And pays us but with age and dust;
Who in the dark and silent grave,
When we have wandered all our ways,
Shuts up the story of our days:
And from which earth, and grave, and dust,
The Lord shall raise me up, I trust.

Sir Walter Ralegh

Crossing the Bar

Sunset and evening star,
    And one clear call for me!
And may there be no moaning of the bar,
    When I put out to sea,

But such a tide as moving seems asleep,
    Too full for sound and foam,
When that which drew from out the boundless deep
    Turns again home.

Twilight and evening bell,
    And after that the dark!
And may there be no sadness of farewell,
    When I embark;

For though from out our bourne of Time and Place
    The flood may bear me far,
I hope to see my Pilot face to face
    When I have crost the bar.

Alfred, Lord Tennyson

Song: "Full fathom five thy father lies"

Full fathom five thy father lies;
    Of his bones are coral made;
Those are pearls that were his eyes:
    Nothing of him that doth fade,
But doth suffer a sea-change
Into something rich and strange:
Sea nymphs hourly ring his knell.
    Ding-dong!
Hark! now I hear them,
    Ding-dong, bell!

William Shakespeare

"My life closed twice before its close"

My life closed twice before its close;
    It yet remains to see
If Immortality unveil
    A third event to me,

So huge, so hopeless to conceive,
    As these that twice befell.
Parting is all we know of heaven,
    And all we need of hell.

Emily Dickinson

Not Waving but Drowning

Nobody heard him, the dead man,
But still he lay moaning:
I was much further out than you thought
And not waving but drowning.

Poor chap, he always loved larking
And now he's dead
It must have been too cold for him his heart gave way,
They said.

Oh, no no no, it was too cold always
(Still the dead one lay moaning)
I was much too far out all my life
And not waving but drowning.

Stevie Smith

Résumé

Razors pain you;
Rivers are damp;
Acids stain you;
And drugs cause cramp.
Guns aren't lawful;
Nooses give;
Gas smells awful;
You might as well live.

Dorothy Parker

Solomon Grundy

Solomon Grundy,
Born on a Monday,
Christened on a Tuesday,
Married on Wednesday,
Took ill on Thursday,
Worse on Friday,
Died on Saturday,
Buried on Sunday.
This is the end
Of Solomon Grundy.

Anon.

On Prince Frederick

Here lies Fred,
Who was alive and is dead:
Had it been his father,
I had much rather;
Had it been his brother,
Still better than another;
Had it been his sister,
No one would have missed her;
Had it been the whole generation,
So much the better for the nation:
But since 'tis only Fred,
Who was alive and is dead,
There's no more to be said.

Anon.

Do Not Go Gentle Into That Good Night

Do not go gentle into that good night,
Old age should burn and rave at close of day;
Rage, rage against the dying of the light.

Though wise men at their end know dark is right,
Because their words had forked no lightning they
Do not go gentle into that good night.

Good men, the last wave by, crying how bright
Their frail deeds might have danced in a green bay,
Rage, rage against the dying of the light.

Wild men who caught and sang the sun in flight,
And learn, too late, they grieved it on its way,
Do not go gentle into that good night.

Grave men, near death, who see with blinding sight
Blind eyes could blaze like meteors and be gay,
Rage, rage against the dying of the light.

And you, my father, there on the sad height,
Curse, bless, me now with your fierce tears, I pray.
Do not go gentle into that good night.
Rage, rage against the dying of the light.

Dylan Thomas

Remember

Remember me when I am gone away,
    Gone far away into the silent land;
    When you can no more hold me by the hand,
Nor I half turn to go yet turning stay.
Remember me when no more day by day
    You tell me of our future that you planned:
    Only remember me; you understand
It will be late to counsel then or pray.
Yet if you should forget me for a while
    And afterwards remember, do not grieve:
    For if the darkness and corruption leave
    A vestige of the thoughts that once I had,
Better by far you should forget and smile
    Than that you should remember and be sad.

Christina Rossetti

Parta Quies

Good-night; ensured release,
Imperishable peace,
   Have these for yours,
While sea abides, and land,
And earth's foundations stand,
   And heaven endures.

When earth's foundations flee,
Nor sky nor land nor sea
   At all is found,
Content you, let them burn:
It is not your concern;
   Sleep on, sleep sound.

A. E. Housman

Afterwards

When the Present has latched its postern behind my
    tremulous stay,
  And the May month flaps its glad green leaves like wings,
Delicate-filmed as new-spun silk, will the neighbours say,
    "He was a man who used to notice such things"?

If it be in the dusk when, like an eyelid's soundless blink,
    The dewfall-hawk comes crossing the shades to alight
Upon the wind-warped upland thorn, a gazer may think,
    "To him this must have been a familiar sight."

If I pass during some nocturnal blackness, mothy and warm,
    When the hedgehog travels furtively over the lawn,
One may say, "He strove that such innocent creatures should
    come to no harm,
    But he could do little for them; and now he is gone."

If, when hearing that I have been stilled at last, they stand
    at the door,
    Watching the full-starred heavens that winter sees,
Will this thought rise on those who will meet my face
    no more,
    "He was one who had an eye for such mysteries"?

And will any say when my bell of quittance is heard in
    the gloom,
    And a crossing breeze cuts a pause in its outrollings,
Till they rise again, as they were a new bell's boom,
    "He hears it not now, but used to notice such things"?

Thomas Hardy

Song: "Stop all the clocks"

Stop all the clocks, cut off the telephone,
Prevent the dog from barking with a juicy bone,
Silence the pianos and with muffled drum
Bring out the coffin, let the mourners come.

Let aeroplanes circle moaning overhead
Scribbling on the sky the message He Is Dead,
Put crêpe bows round the white necks of the public doves,
Let the traffic policemen wear black cotton gloves.

He was my North, my South, my East and West,
My working week and my Sunday rest,
My noon, my midnight, my talk, my song;
I thought that love would last for ever: I was wrong.

The stars are not wanted now: put out every one;
Pack up the moon and dismantle the sun;
Pour away the ocean and sweep up the wood.
For nothing now can ever come to any good.

W. H. Auden

Eden Rock

They are waiting for me somewhere beyond Eden Rock:
My father, twenty-five, in the same suit
Of Genuine Irish Tweed, his terrier Jack
Still two years old and trembling at his feet.

My mother, twenty-three, in a sprigged dress
Drawn at the waist, ribbon in her straw hat,
Has spread the stiff white cloth over the grass.
Her hair, the colour of wheat, takes on the light.

She pours tea from a Thermos, the milk straight
From an old H.P. sauce bottle, a screw
Of paper for a cork; slowly sets out
The same three plates, the tin cups painted blue.

The sky whitens as if lit by three suns.
My mother shades her eyes and looks my way
Over the drifted stream. My father spins
A stone along the water. Leisurely,

They beckon to me from the other bank.
I hear them call, "See where the stream-path is!
Crossing is not as hard as you might think."

I had not thought that it would be like this.

Charles Causley

OF WAR AND PEACE

In Time of "The Breaking of Nations"

Only a man harrowing clods
    In a slow silent walk
With an old horse that stumbles and nods
    Half asleep as they stalk.

Only thin smoke without flame
    From the heaps of couch-grass;
Yet this will go onward the same
    Though Dynasties pass.

Yonder a maid and her wight
    Come whispering by:
War's annals will cloud into night
    Ere their story die.

1915

Thomas Hardy

August 1914

What in our lives is burnt
In the fire of this?
The heart's dear granary?
The much we shall miss?

Three lives hath one life—
Iron, honey, gold.
The gold, the honey gone—
Left is the hard and cold.

Iron are our lives
Molten right through our youth.
A burnt space through ripe fields
A fair mouth's broken tooth.

Isaac Rosenberg

The Soldier

If I should die, think only this of me:
    That there's some corner of a foreign field
That is for ever England. There shall be
    In that rich earth a richer dust concealed;
A dust whom England bore, shaped, made aware,
    Gave, once, her flowers to love, her ways to roam,
A body of England's, breathing English air,
    Washed by the rivers, blest by suns of home.

And think, this heart, all evil shed away,
    A pulse in the eternal mind, no less
        Gives somewhere back the thoughts by England given;
Her sights and sounds; dreams happy as her day;
    And laughter, learnt of friends; and gentleness,
        In hearts at peace, under an English heaven.

Rupert Brooke

To Lucasta, Going to the Wars

Tell me not, sweet, I am unkind,
    That from the nunnery
Of thy chaste breast and quiet mind
    To war and arms I fly.

True, a new mistress now I chase,
    The first foe in the field;
And with a stronger faith embrace
    A sword, a horse, a shield.

Yet this inconstancy is such
    As you too shall adore;
I could not love thee, dear, so much,
    Loved I not honour more.

Sir Richard Lovelace

"Once more unto the breach, dear friends, once more"

Once more unto the breach, dear friends, once more,
Or close the wall up with our English dead!
In peace there's nothing so becomes a man
As modest stillness and humility,
But when the blast of war blows in our ears,
Then imitate the action of the tiger:
Stiffen the sinews, summon up the blood,
Disguise fair nature with hard-favored rage;
Then lend the eye a terrible aspect:
Let it pry through the portage of the head
Like the brass cannon; let the brow o'erwhelm it
As fearfully as doth a gallèd rock
O'erhang and jutty his confounded base,
Swilled with the wild and wasteful ocean.
Now set the teeth and stretch the nostril wide,
Hold hard the breath and bend up every spirit
To his full height! On, on, you noble English,
Whose blood is fet from fathers of war-proof,
Fathers that like so many Alexanders
Have in these parts from morn till even fought
And sheathed their swords for lack of argument.
Dishonor not your mothers; now attest
That those whom you called fathers did beget you!
Be copy now to men of grosser blood
And teach them how to war! And you, good yeomen,
Whose limbs were made in England, show us here
The mettle of your pasture. Let us swear
That you are worth your breeding; which I doubt not.

For there is none of you so mean and base
That hath not noble lustre in your eyes.
I see you stand like greyhounds in the slips,
Straining upon the start. The game's afoot!
Follow your spirit; and upon this charge
Cry "God for Harry! England and Saint George!"

William Shakespeare

War

The victories of mind,
Are won for all mankind;
But war wastes what it wins,
Ends worse than it begins,
And is a game of woes,
Which nations always lose:
Though tyrant tyrant kill,
The slayer liveth still.

Ebenezer Elliott

To His Love

He's gone, and all our plans
   Are useless indeed.
We'll walk no more on Cotswold
   Where the sheep feed
   Quietly and take no heed.

His body that was so quick
   Is not as you
Knew it, on Severn river
   Under the blue
   Driving our small boat through.

You would not know him now . . .
   But still he died
Nobly, so cover him over
   With violets of pride
   Purple from Severn side.

Cover him, cover him soon!
   And with thick-set
Masses of memoried flowers—
   Hide that red wet
   Thing I must somehow forget.

Ivor Gurney

Anthem for Doomed Youth

What passing-bells for these who die as cattle?
    Only the monstrous anger of the guns.
    Only the stuttering rifles' rapid rattle
Can patter out their hasty orisons.
No mockeries for them from prayers or bells,
    Nor any voice of mourning save the choirs,—
The shrill, demented choirs of wailing shells;
    And bugles calling for them from sad shires.

What candles may be held to speed them all?
    Not in the hands of boys, but in their eyes
Shall shine the holy glimmers of good-byes.
    The pallor of girls' brows shall be their pall;
Their flowers the tenderness of silent minds,
And each slow dusk a drawing-down of blinds.

Wilfred Owen

Common Form
1914-1918

If any question why we died,
Tell them, because our fathers lied.

Rudyard Kipling

The Charge of the Light Brigade

I

Half a league, half a league,
　　Half a league onward,
All in the valley of Death
　　Rode the six hundred.
"Forward, the Light Brigade!
Charge for the guns!" he said:
Into the valley of Death
　　Rode the six hundred.

II

"Forward, the Light Brigade!"
Was there a man dismay'd?
Not tho' the soldier knew
　　Some one had blunder'd:
Their's not to make reply,
Their's not to reason why,
Their's but to do and die:
Into the valley of Death
　　Rode the six hundred.

III

Cannon to right of them,
Cannon to left of them,
Cannon in front of them
　　Volley'd and thunder'd;
Storm'd at with shot and shell,
Boldly they rode and well,
Into the jaws of Death,
Into the mouth of Hell
　　Rode the six hundred.

IV

Flash'd all their sabres bare,
Flash'd as they turn'd in air
Sabring the gunners there,
Charging an army, while
  All the world wonder'd:
Plunged in the battery-smoke
Right thro' the line they broke;
Cossack and Russian
Reel'd from the sabre-stroke
  Shatter'd and sunder'd.
Then they rode back, but not,
  Not the six hundred.

V

Cannon to right of them,
Cannon to left of them,
Cannon behind them
  Volley'd and thunder'd;
Storm'd at with shot and shell,
While horse and hero fell,
They that had fought so well
Came thro' the jaws of Death,
Back from the mouth of Hell,
All that was left of them,
  Left of six hundred.

VI

When can their glory fade?
O the wild charge they made!
  All the world wonder'd.
Honour the charge they made!
Honour the Light Brigade,
  Noble six hundred!

Alfred, Lord Tennyson

Dulce et Decorum Est

Bent double, like old beggars under sacks,
Knock-kneed, coughing like hags, we cursed through sludge,
Till on the haunting flares we turned our backs
And towards our distant rest began to trudge.
Men marched asleep. Many had lost their boots
But limped on, blood-shod. All went lame; all blind;
Drunk with fatigue; deaf even to the hoots
Of tired, outstripped Five-Nines that dropped behind.

Gas! GAS! Quick, boys!—An ecstasy of fumbling,
Fitting the clumsy helmets just in time;
But someone still was yelling out and stumbling
And flound'ring like a man in fire or lime . . .
Dim, through the misty panes and thick green light,
As under a green sea, I saw him drowning.

In all my dreams, before my helpless sight,
He plunges at me, guttering, choking, drowning.

If in some smothering dreams you too could pace
Behind the wagon that we flung him in,
And watch the white eyes writhing in his face,
His hanging face, like a devil's sick of sin;
If you could hear, at every jolt, the blood
Come gargling from the froth-corrupted lungs,
Obscene as cancer, bitter as the cud
Of vile, incurable sores on innocent tongues,—
My friend, you would not tell with such high zest
To children ardent for some desperate glory,
The old Lie: Dulce et decorum est
Pro patria mori.

Wilfred Owen

Peace

My soul, there is a country
   Far beyond the stars,
Where stands a wingèd sentry
   All skilful in the wars:
There above noise and danger
   Sweet Peace sits crowned with smiles,
And One born in a manger
   Commands the beauteous files.
He is thy gracious friend
   And—O my soul, awake!—
Did in pure love descend
   To die here for thy sake.
If thou canst get but thither,
   There grows the flower of Peace,
The Rose that cannot wither,
   Thy fortress, and thy ease.
Leave then thy foolish ranges
   For none can thee secure,
But one who never changes,
   Thy God, thy life, thy cure.

Henry Vaughan

Christmas: 1924

"Peace upon Earth!" was said. We sing it,
And pay a million priests to bring it.
After two thousand years of mass
We've got as far as poison-gas.

Thomas Hardy

For the Fallen
(SEPTEMBER 1914)

With proud thanksgiving, a mother for her children,
England mourns for her dead across the sea.
Flesh of her flesh they were, spirit of her spirit,
Fallen in the cause of the free.

Solemn the drums thrill: Death august and royal
Sings sorrow up into immortal spheres.
There is music in the midst of desolation
And a glory that shines upon our tears.

They went with songs to the battle, they were young,
Straight of limb, true of eye, steady and aglow.
They were staunch to the end against odds uncounted,
They fell with their faces to the foe.

They shall grow not old, as we that are left grow old:
Age shall not weary them, nor the years condemn.
At the going down of the sun and in the morning
We will remember them.

They mingle not with their laughing comrades again;
They sit no more at familiar tables of home;
They have no lot in our labour of the day-time;
They sleep beyond England's foam.

But where our desires are and our hopes profound,
Felt as a well-spring that is hidden from sight,
To the innermost heart of their own land they are known
As the stars are known to the Night;

As the stars that shall be bright when we are dust,
Moving in marches upon the heavenly plain,
As the stars that are starry in the time of our darkness,
To the end, to the end, they remain.

Laurence Binyon

In A Notebook

There was a river overhung with trees
With wooden houses built along its shallows
From which the morning sun drew up a haze
And the gyrations of the early swallows
Paid no attention to the gentle breeze
Which spoke discreetly from the weeping willows.
There was a jetty by the forest clearing
Where a small boat was tugging at its mooring.

And night still lingered underneath the eaves.
In the dark houseboats families were stirring
And Chinese soup was cooked on charcoal stoves.
Then one by one there came into the clearing
Mothers and daughters bowed beneath their sheaves.
The silent children gathered round me staring
And the shy soldiers setting out for battle
Asked for a cigarette and laughed a little.

From low canoes old men laid out their nets
While on the bank young boys with lines were fishing.
The wicker traps were drawn up by their floats.
The girls stood waist-deep in the river washing
Or tossed the day's rice on enamel plates
And I sat drinking bitter coffee wishing
The tide would turn to bring me to my senses
After the pleasant war and the evasive answers.

There was a river overhung with trees.
The girls stood waist-deep in the river washing,
And night still lingered underneath the eaves
While on the bank young boys with lines were fishing.
Mothers and daughters bowed beneath their sheaves
While I sat drinking bitter coffee wishing—
And the tide turned and brought me to my senses.
The pleasant war brought the unpleasant answers:

The villages are burnt, the cities void;
The morning light has left the river view;
The distant followers have been dismayed;
And I'm afraid, reading this passage now;
That everything I knew has been destroyed
By those whom I admired but never knew;
The laughing soldiers fought to their defeat
And I'm afraid most of my friends are dead.

James Fenton

The Last Day

When the last day comes
a ploughman in Europe will look over his shoulder
and see the hard furrows of earth
finally behind him, he will watch his shadow
run back into his spine.

It will be morning
for the first time, and the long night
will be seen for what it is,
a black flag trembling in the sunlight.
On the last day

our stories will be rewritten
each from the end,
and each will end the same;
you will hear the fields and rivers clap
and under the trees

old bones
will cover themselves with flesh;
spears, bullets, will pluck themselves
from wounds already healed,
women will clasp their sons as men

and men will look
into their palms and find them empty;
there will be time
for us to say the right things at last,
to look into our enemy's face

and see ourselves,
forgiven now, before the books flower in flames,
the mirrors return our faces,
and everything is stripped from us,
even our names.

Kevin Hart

TO READ ALOUD

If—

If you can keep your head when all about you
    Are losing theirs and blaming it on you,
If you can trust yourself when all men doubt you,
    But make allowance for their doubting too;
If you can wait and not be tired by waiting,
    Or being lied about, don't deal in lies,
Or being hated, don't give way to hating,
    And yet don't look too good, nor talk too wise:

If you can dream—and not make dreams your master;
    If you can think—and not make thoughts your aim;
If you can meet with Triumph and Disaster
    And treat those two impostors just the same;
If you can bear to hear the truth you've spoken
    Twisted by knaves to make a trap for fools,
Or watch the things you gave your life to, broken,
    And stoop and build 'em up with worn-out tools:

If you can make one heap of all your winnings
    And risk it on one turn of pitch-and-toss,
And lose, and start again at your beginnings
    And never breathe a word about your loss;
If you can force your heart and nerve and sinew
    To serve your turn long after they are gone,
And so hold on when there is nothing in you
    Except the Will which says to them: "Hold on!"

If you can talk with crowds and keep your virtue,
   Or walk with Kings—nor lose the common touch,
If neither foes nor loving friends can hurt you,
   If all men count with you, but none too much;
If you can fill the unforgiving minute
   With sixty seconds' worth of distance run,
Yours is the Earth and everything that's in it,
   And—which is more—you'll be a Man, my son!

Rudyard Kipling

"I'm nobody! Who are you?"

I'm nobody! Who are you?
Are you nobody, too?
Then there's a pair of us—don't tell!
They'd banish us you know.

How dreary to be somebody!
How public, like a frog
To tell your name the livelong day
To an admiring bog!

Emily Dickinson

"All the world's a stage"

All the world's a stage,
And all the men and women merely players:
They have their exits and their entrances;
And one man in his time plays many parts,
His acts being seven ages. At first the infant,
Mewling and puking in the nurse's arms.
And then the whining schoolboy, with his satchel,
And shining morning face, creeping like snail
Unwillingly to school. And then the lover,
Sighing like furnace, with a woeful ballad
Made to his mistress' eyebrow. Then a soldier,
Full of strange oaths, and bearded like the pard,
Jealous in honour, sudden and quick in quarrel,
Seeking the bubble reputation
Even in the cannon's mouth. And then the justice,
In fair round belly with good capon lined,
With eyes severe and beard of formal cut,
Full of wise saws and modern instances;
And so he plays his part. The sixth age shifts
Into the lean and slippered pantaloon,
With spectacles on nose, and pouch on side;
His youthful hose, well saved, a world too wide
For his shrunk shank; and his big manly voice,
Turning again toward childish treble, pipes
And whistles in his sound. Last scene of all,
That ends this strange eventful history,
Is second childishness and mere oblivion,
Sans teeth, sans eyes, sans taste, sans everything.

William Shakespeare

Impromptu on Charles II

God bless our good and gracious King,
Whose promise none relies on;
Who never said a foolish thing,
Nor ever did a wise one.

John Wilmot, Earl of Rochester

Epigram

<small>ENGRAVED ON THE COLLAR OF A DOG WHICH I GAVE TO HIS ROYAL HIGHNESS</small>

I am his Highness' Dog at Kew:
Pray tell me, sir, whose dog are you?

Alexander Pope

Lord Finchley

Lord Finchley tried to mend the Electric Light
Himself. It struck him dead: And serve him right!
It is the business of the wealthy man
To give employment to the artisan.

Hilaire Belloc

The Song of the Lower Classes

We plough and sow—we're so very, very low,
    That we delve in the dirty clay,
Till we bless the plain—with the golden grain,
    And the vale with the fragrant hay,
Our place we know,—we're so very low,
    'Tis down at the landlord's feet:
We're not too low—the bread to grow,
    But too low the bread to eat.

Down, down we go,—we're so very low,
    To the hell of the deep sunk mines,
But we gather the proudest gems that glow,
    When the crown of a despot shines.
And whenever he lacks—upon our backs
    Fresh loads he deigns to lay:
We're far too low to vote the tax,
    But not too low to pay.

We're low—we're low—mere rabble, we know
    But, at our plastic power,
The mould at the lordling's feet will grow
    Into palace and church and tower.
Then prostrate fall—in the rich man's hall,
    And cringe at the rich man's door;
We're not too low to build the wall,
    But too low to tread the floor.

We're low—we're low—we're very very low,
    Yet from our fingers glide
The silken flow—and the robes that glow
    Round the limbs of the sons of pride,
And what we get—and what we give—
    We know, and we know our share;
We're not too low the cloth to weave,
    But too low the Cloth to wear!

We're low—we're low—we're very very low,
    And yet when the trumpets ring,
The thrust of a poor man's arm will go
    Thro' the heart of the proudest King.
We're low—we're low—our place we know,
    We're only the rank and file,
We're not too low—to kill the foe,
    But too low to touch the spoil.

Ernest Jones

She Was Poor, but She Was Honest

She was poor, but she was honest,
    Victim of the squire's whim.
First he loved her, then he left her,
    And she lost her honest name.

Then she ran away to London,
    For to hide her grief and shame,
There she met another squire,
    And she lost her name again.

See her riding in her carriage,
    In the Park and all so gay,
All the nibs and nobby persons
    Come to pass the time of day.

See the little old-world village
    Where her aged parents live,
Drinking the champagne she sends them,
    But they never can forgive.

In the rich man's arms she flutters,
    Like a bird with broken wing,
First he loved her, then he left her,
    And she hasn't got a ring.

See him in the splendid mansion,
  Entertaining with the best,
While the girl as he has ruined,
  Entertains a sordid guest.

See him in the House of Commons,
  Making laws to put down crime,
While the victim of his passions
  Trails her way through mud and slime.

See her on the bridge at midnight,
  Crying, "Farewell, faithless love!"
There's scream, a splash—Good Heavens!
  What is she a-doing of?

Then they dragged her from the river,
  Water from her clothes they wrung,
They all thought that she was drownded,
  But the corpse got up and sung:

"It's the same the whole world over,
  It's the poor as gets the blame,
It's the rich as gets the pleasure—
  Ain't it all a blooming shame?"

Anon.

The King's Breakfast

The King asked
The Queen, and
The Queen asked
The Dairymaid:
"Could we have some butter for
The Royal slice of bread?"
The Queen asked
The Dairymaid,
The Dairymaid
Said: "Certainly,
I'll go and tell
The cow
Now
Before she goes to bed."

The Dairymaid
She curtsied,
And went and told
The Alderney:
"Don't forget the butter for
The Royal slice of bread."
The Alderney
Said sleepily:
"You'd better tell
His Majesty
That many people nowadays
Like marmalade
Instead."

The Dairymaid
Said: "Fancy!"
And went to
Her Majesty.
She curtsied to the Queen, and
She turned a little red:
"Excuse me,
Your Majesty,
For taking of
The liberty,
But marmalade is tasty, if
It's very
Thickly
Spread."

The Queen said:
"Oh!"
And went to
His Majesty:
"Talking of the butter for
The Royal slice of bread,
Many people
Think that
Marmalade
Is nicer.
Would you like to try a little
Marmalade
Instead?"

The King said:
"Bother!"
And then he said:
"Oh, deary me!"
The King sobbed: "Oh, deary me!"
And went back to bed.
"Nobody,"
He whimpered,
"Could call me
A fussy man;
I *only* want
A little bit
Of butter for
My bread!"

The Queen said:
"There, there!"
And went to
The Dairymaid.
The Dairymaid
Said: "There, there!"
And went to the shed.
The cow said:
"There, there!
I didn't really
Mean it;
Here's milk for his porringer
And butter for his bread."

The Queen took
The butter
And brought it to
His Majesty;
The King said:
"Butter, eh?"
And bounced out of bed.
"Nobody," he said:
As he kissed her
Tenderly,
"Nobody," he said,
As he slid down
The banisters,
"Nobody,
My darling,
Could call me
A fussy man—
BUT
I do like a little bit of butter to my bread!"

A. A. Milne

A Nightmare

When you're lying awake with a dismal headache, and repose
    is taboo'd by anxiety,
I conceive you may use any language you choose to indulge
    in without impropriety;
For your brain is on fire—the bedclothes conspire of usual
    slumber to plunder you:
First your counterpane goes and uncovers your toes, and your
    sheet slips demurely from under you;
Then the blanketing tickles—you feel like mixed pickles, so
    terribly sharp is the pricking,
And you're hot, and you're cross, and you tumble and toss till
    there's nothing 'twixt you and the ticking.
Then the bedclothes all creep to the ground in a heap, and
    you pick 'em all up in a tangle;
Next your pillow resigns and politely declines to remain at
    its usual angle!
Well, you get some repose in the form of a doze, with hot
    eyeballs and head ever aching,
But your slumbering teems with such horrible dreams that
    you'd very much better be waking;
For you dream you are crossing the Channel, and tossing
    about in a steamer from Harwich,
Which is something between a large bathing-machine and a
    very small second-class carriage;
And you're giving a treat (penny ice and cold meat) to a
    party of friends and relations—
They're a ravenous horde—and they all came on board at
    Sloane Square and South Kensington Stations.
And bound on that journey you find your attorney (who
    started that morning from Devon);

He's a bit undersized, and you don't feel surprised when he
    tells you he's only eleven.
Well, you're driving like mad with this singular lad (by the
    bye the ship's now a four-wheeler),
And you're playing round games, and he calls you bad names
    when you tell him that "ties pay the dealer";
But this you can't stand, so you throw up your hand, and you
    find you're as cold as an icicle,
In your shirt and your socks (the black silk with gold clocks),
    crossing Salisbury Plain on a bicycle:
And he and the crew are on bicycles too—which they've
    somehow or other invested in—
And he's telling the tars all the particulars of a company he's
    interested in—
It's a scheme of devices, to get at low prices, all goods from
    cough mixtures to cables
(Which tickled the sailors) by treating retailers, as though
    they were all vegetables—
You get a good spadesman to plant a small tradesman (first
    take off his boots with a boot-tree),
And his legs will take root, and his fingers will shoot, and
    they'll blossom and bud like a fruit-tree—
From the greengrocer tree you get grapes and green pea,
    cauliflower, pineapple, and cranberries,
While the pastry-cook plant cherry-brandy will grant—apple
    puffs, and three-corners, and banberries—
The shares are a penny, and ever so many are taken by
    ROTHSCHILD and BARING,
And just as a few are allotted to you, you awake with a
    shudder despairing—

You're a regular wreck, with a crick in your neck, and no
 wonder you snore, for your head's on the floor, and you've
 needles and pins from your soles to your shins, and your
 flesh is a-creep, for your left leg's asleep, and you've cramp
 in your toes, and a fly on your nose, and some fluff in your
 lung, and a feverish tongue, and a thirst that's intense, and
 a general sense that you haven't been sleeping in clover;
But the darkness has passed, and it's daylight at last, and the
 night has been long—ditto, ditto my song—and thank
 goodness they're both of them over!

W. S. Gilbert

Three Ghostesses

Three little ghostesses,
Sitting on postesses,
Eating buttered toastesses,
Greasing their fistesses,
Up to their wristesses.
Oh, what beastesses
To make such feastesses!

Anon.

"There is pleasure in the wet, wet clay"

There is pleasure in the wet, wet clay,
When the artist's hand is potting it.
There is pleasure in the wet, wet lay,
When the poet's pad is blotting it.
There is pleasure in the shine of your
    picture on the line
At the Royal Acade-my
But the pleasure felt in these is as chalk
    to Cheddar cheese
When it comes to a well made Lie.
To a quite unwreckable Lie,
To a most impeccable Lie!
To a water-tight, fire-proof, angle-iron,
    sunk-hinge, time-lock, steel-faced Lie!
Not a private hansom Lie,
But a pair-and-brougham Lie,
Not a little-place-at-Tooting, but a
    country-house-with-shooting
And a ring-fence-deer-park Lie.

Rudyard Kipling

"Great things are done"

Great things are done when men and mountains meet;
This is not done by jostling in the street.

William Blake

Macavity: The Mystery Cat

Macavity's a Mystery Cat: he's called the Hidden Paw—
For he's the master criminal who can defy the Law.
He's the bafflement of Scotland Yard, the Flying Squad's
    despair:
For when they reach the scene of crime—*Macavity's not there!*

Macavity, Macavity, there's no one like Macavity,
He's broken every human law, he breaks the law of gravity.
His powers of levitation would make a fakir stare,
And when you reach the scene of crime—*Macavity's not there!*
You may seek him in the basement, you may look up
    in the air—
But I tell you once and once again, *Macavity's not there!*

Macavity's a ginger cat, he's very tall and thin;
You would know him if you saw him, for his eyes are
    sunken in.
His brow is deeply lined with thought, his head is
    highly domed;
His coat is dusty from neglect, his whiskers are uncombed.
He sways his head from side to side, with movements
    like a snake;
And when you think he's half asleep, he's always wide awake.

Macavity, Macavity, there's no one like Macavity,
For he's a fiend in feline shape, a monster of depravity.
You may meet him in a by-street, you may see him
    in the square—
But when a crime's discovered, then *Macavity's not there!*

He's outwardly respectable. (They say he cheats at cards.)
And his footprints are not found in any file of
    Scotland Yard's.

And when the larder's looted, or the jewel-case is rifled,
Or when the milk is missing, or another Peke's been stifled,
Or the greenhouse glass is broken, and the trellis past repair—
Ay, there's the wonder of the thing! *Macavity's not there!*

And when the Foreign Office find a Treaty's gone astray,
Or the Admiralty lose some plans and drawings by the way,
There may be a scrap of paper in the hall or on the stair—
But it's useless to investigate—*Macavity's not there!*
And when the loss has been disclosed, the Secret Service say:
"It *must* have been Macavity!"—but he's a mile away.
You'll be sure to find him resting, or a-licking of his thumbs,
Or engaged in doing complicated long division sums.

Macavity, Macavity, there's no one like Macavity,
There never was a Cat of such deceitfulness and suavity.
He always has an alibi, and one or two to spare:
At whatever time the deed took place—
   MACAVITY WASN'T THERE!
And they say that all the Cats whose wicked deeds are
   widely known
(I might mention Mungojerrie, I might mention Griddlebone)
Are nothing more than agents for the Cat who all the time
Just controls their operations: the Napoleon of Crime!

T. S. Eliot

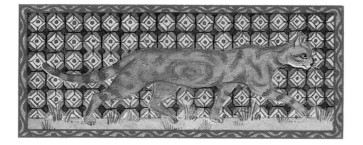

The Ruined Maid

"O 'melia, my dear, this does everything crown!
Who could have supposed I should meet you in Town?
And whence such fair garments, such prosperi-ty?"—
"O didn't you know I'd been ruined?" said she.

—"You left us in tatters, without shoes or socks,
Tired of digging potatoes, and spudding up docks;
And now you've gay bracelets and bright feathers three!"—
"Yes: that's how we dress when we're ruined," said she.

—"At home in the barton you said 'thee' and 'thou',
And 'thik oon', and 'theäs oon', and 't'other'; but now
Your talking quite fits 'ee for high compa-ny!"—
"Some polish is gained with one's ruin," said she.

—"Your hands were like paws then, your face blue and bleak
But now I'm bewitched by your delicate cheek,
And your little gloves fit as on any la-dy!"—
"We never do work when we're ruined," said she.

—"You used to call home-life a hag-ridden dream,
And you'd sigh, and you'd sock; but at present you seem
To know not of megrims or melancho-ly!"—
"True. One's pretty lively when ruined," said she.

—"I wish I had feathers, a fine sweeping gown,
And a delicate face, and could strut about Town!"—
"My dear—a raw country girl, such as you be,
Cannot quite expect that. You ain't ruined," said she.

Thomas Hardy

Abou Ben Adhem

Abou Ben Adhem (may his tribe increase!)
Awoke one night from a deep dream of peace,
And saw, within the moonlight in his room,
Making it rich, and like a lily in bloom,
An angel writing in a book of gold:—
Exceeding peace had made Ben Adhem bold,
And to the presence in the room he said,
   "What writest thou?"—The vision raised its head,
And with a look made of all sweet accord,
Answered, "The names of those who love the Lord."
"And is mine one?" said Abou. "Nay, not so,"
Replied the angel. Abou spoke more low,
But cheerly still; and said, "I pray thee, then,
Write me as one that loves his fellow men."

   The angel wrote, and vanished. The next night
It came again with a great wakening light,
And showed the names whom love of God had blest,
And lo! Ben Adhem's name led all the rest.

Leigh Hunt

Biby's Epitaph

A muvver was barfin' 'er biby one night,
The youngest of ten and a tiny young mite,
The muvver was poor and the biby was thin,
Only a skelington covered in skin;
The muvver turned rahnd for the soap off the rack,
She was but a moment, but when she turned back,
The biby was gorn; and in anguish she cried,
"Oh, where is my biby?"—The angels replied:

"Your biby 'as fell dahn the plug-'ole,
Your biby 'as gorn dahn the plug;
The poor little thing was so skinny and thin
'E oughter been barfed in a jug;
Your biby is perfeckly 'appy,
'E won't need a barf any more,
Your biby 'as fell dahn the plug-'ole,
Not lorst, but gorn before."

Anon.

Cargoes

Quinquireme of Nineveh from distant Ophir
Rowing home to haven in sunny Palestine,
With a cargo of ivory,
And apes and peacocks,
Sandalwood, cedarwood, and sweet white wine.

Stately Spanish galleon coming from the Isthmus,
Dipping through the Tropics by the palm-green shores,
With a cargo of diamonds,
Emeralds, amethysts,
Topazes, and cinnamon, and gold moidores.

Dirty British coaster with a salt-caked smoke stack
Butting through the Channel in the mad March days,
With a cargo of Tyne coal,
Road-rail, pig-lead,
Firewood, iron-ware, and cheap tin trays.

John Masefield

The Bells

I

Hear the sledges with the bells—
    Silver bells!
What a world of merriment their melody foretells!
    How they tinkle, tinkle, tinkle,
      In the icy air of night!
    While the stars that oversprinkle
    All the heavens, seem to twinkle
      With a crystalline delight;
    Keeping time, time, time,
    In a sort of Runic rhyme,
To the tintinnabulation that so musically wells
    From the bells, bells, bells, bells,
      Bells, bells, bells—
From the jingling and the tinkling of the bells.

II

Hear the mellow wedding bells,
    Golden bells!
What a world of happiness their harmony foretells!
    Through the balmy air of night
    How they ring out their delight!
      From the molten-golden notes,
        And all in tune,
      What a liquid ditty floats
To the turtle-dove that listens, while she gloats
      On the moon!
    Oh, from out the sounding cells,
What a gush of euphony voluminously wells!
      How it swells!
      How it dwells
    On the Future! how it tells

Of the rapture that impels
To the swinging and the ringing
Of the bells, bells, bells,
Of the bells, bells, bells, bells,
Bells, bells, bells—
To the rhyming and the chiming of the bells!

III

Hear the loud alarum bells—
Brazen bells!
What a tale of terror, now, their turbulency tells!
In the startled ear of night
How they scream out their affright!
Too much horrified to speak,
They can only shriek, shriek,
Out of tune,
In a clamorous appealing to the mercy of the fire,
In a mad expostulation with the deaf and frantic fire,
Leaping higher, higher, higher,
With a desperate desire,
And a resolute endeavor,
Now—now to sit or never,
By the side of the pale-faced moon.

Oh, the bells, bells, bells!
What a tale their terror tells
　　Of Despair!
How they clang, and clash, and roar!
What a horror they outpour
On the bosom of the palpitating air!
　　Yet the ear it fully knows,
　　　By the twanging,
　　　And the clanging,
　　How the danger ebbs and flows:
　Yet the ear distinctly tells,
　　　In the jangling,
　　　And the wrangling,
　How the danger sinks and swells,
By the sinking or the swelling in the anger of the bells—
　　　Of the bells—
　Of the bells, bells, bells, bells,
　　Bells, bells, bells—
In the clamor and the clanger of the bells!

IV

Hear the tolling of the bells—
　　Iron bells!
What a world of solemn thought their monody compels!
　In the silence of the night,
　How we shiver with affright
At the melancholy menace of their tone!
　For every sound that floats
　From the rust within their throats
　　Is a groan.
　And the people—ah, the people—
　They that dwell up in the steeple,
　　All alone,
And who, tolling, tolling, tolling,
　In that muffled monotone,

Feel a glory in so rolling
   On the human heart a stone—
They are neither man nor woman—
They are neither brute nor human—
    They are Ghouls:
  And their king it is who tolls;
  And he rolls, rolls, rolls,
    Rolls
  A paean from the bells!
And his merry bosom swells
  With the paean of the bells!
And he dances, and he yells;
Keeping time, time, time,
In a sort of Runic rhyme,
  To the paean of the bells—
    Of the bells:
Keeping time, time, time,
In a sort of Runic rhyme,
  To the throbbing of the bells—
Of the bells, bells, bells—
  To the sobbing of the bells;
Keeping time, time, time,
  As he knells, knells, knells,
In a happy Runic rhyme,
  To the rolling of the bells—
Of the bells, bells, bells:
  To the tolling of the bells,
Of the bells, bells, bells, bells—
  Bells, bells, bells—
To the moaning and the groaning of the bells.

Edgar Allan Poe

Waltzing Matilda

Once a jolly swagman camped beside a billabong,
  Under the shade of a coolibah tree,
And he sang as he sat and waited while his billy boiled,
  "Who'll come a-waltzing Matilda with me—
Waltzing Matilda, waltzing Matilda, who'll come
    a-waltzing Matilda with me?"
And he sang as he sat and waited while his billy boiled,
  "Who'll come a-waltzing Matilda with me?"

Down came a jumbuck to drink at the billabong,
  Up jumped the swagman and grabbed him with glee,
And he sang, as he stowed it away in his tucker-bag,
  "Who'll come a-waltzing Matilda with me?
Waltzing Matilda, waltzing Matilda, who'll come
    a-waltzing Matilda with me?"
And he sang as he stowed it away in his tucker-bag,
  "Who'll come a-waltzing Matilda with me?"

Up came the squatter, riding on his thoroughbred,
  Down came the troopers—one, two, three—
"Whose is the jumbuck, you've got in your tucker-bag?
  You'll come a-waltzing Matilda with me.
Waltzing Matilda, waltzing Matilda, who'll come
    a-waltzing Matilda with me?
Whose is the jumbuck you've got in your tucker-bag?
  You'll come a-waltzing Matilda with me."

Up jumped the swagman, and sprang into the billabong,
  "You'll never take me alive!" said he.
And his ghost can be heard, as we pass beside the
    billabong,
  "Who'll come a-waltzing Matilda with me?
Waltzing Matilda, waltzing Matilda,
  Who'll come a-waltzing Matilda with me?"
And his ghost can be heard as we pass beside the billabong,
  "Who'll come a-waltzing Matilda with me?"

A. B. "Banjo" Paterson

Brahma

If the wild bowler thinks he bowls,
  Or if the batsman thinks he's bowled,
They know not, poor misguided souls,
  They too shall perish unconsoled.
I am the batsman and the bat,
  I am the bowler and the ball,
The umpire, the pavilion cat,
  The roller, pitch, and stumps, and all.

Andrew Lang

Symphony in Yellow

An omnibus across the bridge
   Crawls like a yellow butterfly,
   And, here and there, a passer-by
Shows like a little restless midge.

Big barges full of yellow hay
   Are moored against the shadowy wharf,
   And, like a yellow silken scarf,
The thick fog hangs along the quay.

The yellow leaves begin to fade
   And flutter from the Temple elms,
   And at my feet the pale green Thames
Lies like a rod of rippled jade.

Oscar Wilde

TO READ QUIETLY

"To see a World in a Grain of Sand"

To see a World in a Grain of Sand
And a Heaven in a Wild Flower,
Hold Infinity in the palm of your hand
And Eternity in an hour.

William Blake

"Flower in the crannied wall"

Flower in the crannied wall,
I pluck you out of the crannies,
I hold you here, root and all in my hand,
Little flower—but *if* I could understand
What you are, root and all, and all in all,
I should know what God and man is.

Alfred, Lord Tennyson

Cock-Crow

Out of the wood of thoughts that grows by night
To be cut down by the sharp axe of light,—
Out of the night, two cocks together crow,
Cleaving the darkness with a silver blow:
And bright before my eyes twin trumpeters stand,
Heralds of splendour, one at either hand,
Each facing each as in a coat of arms:
The milkers lace their boots up at the farms.

Edward Thomas

A Mill

Two leaps the water from its race
Made to the brook below;
The first leap it was curving glass,
The second bounding snow.

William Allingham

Heaven-Haven

A NUN TAKES THE VEIL

I have desired to go
　　Where springs not fail,
To fields where flies no sharp and sided hail
　　And a few lilies blow.

And I have asked to be
　　Where no storms come,
Where the green swell is in the havens dumb,
　　And out of the swing of the sea.

Gerard Manley Hopkins

Bitter-Sweet

Ah my dear angry Lord,
Since thou dost love, yet strike;
Cast down, yet help afford;
Sure I will do the like.

I will complain, yet praise;
I will bewail, approve;
And all my sour-sweet days
I will lament, and love.

George Herbert

Afternoon Service at Mellstock

(CIRCA 1850)

On afternoons of drowsy calm
　　We stood in the panelled pew,
Singing one-voiced a Tate-and-Brady psalm
　　To the tune of 'Cambridge New'.

We watched the elms, we watched the rooks,
　　The clouds upon the breeze,
Between the whiles of glancing at our books,
　　And swaying like the trees.

So mindless were those outpourings!—
　　Though I am not aware
That I have gained by subtle thought on things
　　Since we stood psalming there.

Thomas Hardy

"I give you the end of a golden string"

I give you the end of a golden string:
Only wind it into a ball,
It will lead you into Heaven's Gate
Built in Jerusalem's wall

William Blake

The World

Great, wide, beautiful, wonderful World,
With the wonderful water round you curled,
And the wonderful grass upon your breast—
World, you are beautifully drest.

The wonderful air is over me,
And the wonderful wind is shaking the tree,
It walks on the water, and whirls the mills,
And talks to itself on the tops of the hills.

You friendly Earth, how far do you go,
With the wheatfields that nod and the rivers that flow,
With cities and gardens, and cliffs, and isles,
And people upon you for thousands of miles?

Ah, you are so great, and I am so small,
I tremble to think of you, World, at all;
And yet, when I said my prayers today,
A whisper inside me seemed to say,
"You are more than the Earth, though you are such a dot:
You can love and think, and the Earth cannot."

William Brighty Rands

Above the Dock

Above the quiet dock in midnight,
Tangled in the tall mast's corded height,
Hangs the moon. What seemed so far away
Is but a child's balloon, forgotten after play.

T. E. Hulme

"who knows if the moon's a balloon"

who knows if the moon's
a balloon,coming out of a keen city
in the sky—filled with pretty people?
(and if you and i should

get into it,if they
should take me and take you into their balloon,
why then
we'd go up higher with all the pretty people

than houses and steeples and clouds:
go sailing
away and away sailing into a keen
city which nobody's ever visited,where

always
     it's
        Spring)and everyone's
in love and flowers pick themselves

E. E. Cummings

Spell of Creation

Within the flower there lies a seed,
Within the seed there springs a tree,
Within the tree there spreads a wood.

In the wood there burns a fire,
And in the fire there melts a stone,
Within the stone a ring of iron.

Within the ring there lies an O
Within the O there looks an eye,
In the eye there swims a sea,

And in the sea reflected sky,
And in the sky there shines the sun,
Within the sun a bird of gold.

Within the bird there beats a heart,
And from the heart there flows a song,
And in the song there sings a word.

In the word there speaks a world,
A word of joy, a world of grief,
From joy and grief there springs my love.

Oh love, my love, there springs a world,
And on the world there shines a sun
And in the sun there burns a fire,

Within the fire consumes my heart
And in my heart there beats a bird,
And in the bird there wakes an eye,

Within the eye, earth, sea and sky,
Earth, sky and sea within an O
Lie like the seed within the flower.

Kathleen Raine

Tall Nettles

Tall nettles cover up, as they have done
These many springs, the rusty harrow, the plough
Long worn out, and the roller made of stone:
Only the elm butt tops the nettles now.

This corner of the farmyard I like most:
As well as any bloom upon a flower
I like the dust on the nettles, never lost
Except to prove the sweetness of a shower.

Edward Thomas

151

Ozymandias

I met a traveller from an antique land
Who said: Two vast and trunkless legs of stone
Stand in the desert . . . Near them, on the sand,
Half sunk, a shattered visage lies, whose frown,
And wrinkled lip, and sneer of cold command,
Tell that its sculptor well those passions read
Which yet survive, stamped on these lifeless things,
The hand that mocked them, and the heart that fed:
And on the pedestal these words appear:
"My name is Ozymandias, king of kings:
Look on my works, ye Mighty, and despair!"
Nothing beside remains. Round the decay
Of that colossal wreck, boundless and bare
The lone and level sands stretch far away.

Percy Bysshe Shelley

"A man said to the universe"

A man said to the universe:
"Sir, I exist!"
"However," replied the universe,
"The fact has not created in me
A sense of obligation."

Stephen Crane

A Vision

I lost the love of heaven above
I spurned the lust of earth below
I felt the sweets of fancied love
And hell itself my only foe

I lost earth's joys but felt the glow
Of heaven's flame abound in me
Till loveliness and I did grow
The bard of immortality

I loved but woman fell away
I hid me from her faded fame
I snatched the sun's eternal ray
And wrote till earth was but a name

In every language upon earth
On every shore, o'er every sea,
I gave my name immortal birth,
And kept my spirit with the free

John Clare

Ode to a Nightingale

My heart aches, and a drowsy numbness pains
    My sense, as though of hemlock I had drunk,
Or emptied some dull opiate to the drains
    One minute past, and Lethe-wards had sunk:
'Tis not through envy of thy happy lot,
    But being too happy in thy happiness,
        That thou, light-wingèd Dryad of the trees,
            In some melodious plot
    Of beechen green, and shadows numberless,
        Singest of summer in full-throated ease.

O for a draught of vintage! that hath been
    Cooled a long age in the deep-delvèd earth,
Tasting of Flora and the country-green,
    Dance, and Provençal song, and sunburnt mirth!
O for a beaker full of the warm South!
    Full of the true, the blushful Hippocrene,
        With beaded bubbles winking at the brim,
            And purple-stainèd mouth;
    That I might drink, and leave the world unseen,
    And with thee fade away into the forest dim:

Fade far away, dissolve, and quite forget
    What thou among the leaves hast never known,
The weariness, the fever, and the fret
    Here, where men sit and hear each other groan;
Where palsy shakes a few, sad, last grey hairs,
    Where youth grows pale, and spectre-thin, and dies;
        Where but to think is to be full of sorrow
            And leaden-eyed despairs;
    Where Beauty cannot keep her lustrous eyes,
    Or new Love pine at them beyond to-morrow.

Away! away! for I will fly to thee,
　　Not charioted by Bacchus and his pards,
But on the viewless wings of Poesy,
　　Though the dull brain perplexes and retards:
Already with thee! tender is the night,
　　And haply the Queen-Moon is on her throne,
　　　　Clustered around by all her starry Fays;
　　　　　　But here there is no light,
　　Save what from heaven is with the breezes blown
　　　　Through verdurous glooms and winding mossy ways.

I cannot see what flowers are at my feet,
　　Nor what soft incense hangs upon the boughs,
But, in embalmèd darkness, guess each sweet
　　Wherewith the seasonable month endows
The grass, the thicket, and the fruit-tree wild;
　　White hawthorn, and the pastoral eglantine;
　　　　Fast fading violets covered up in leaves;
　　　　　　And mid-May's eldest child,
　　The coming musk-rose, full of dewy wine,
　　　　The murmurous haunt of flies on summer eves.

Darkling I listen; and for many a time
　　I have been half in love with easeful Death,
Called him soft names in many a musèd rhyme,
　　To take into the air my quiet breath;
Now more than ever seems it rich to die,
　　To cease upon the midnight with no pain,
　　　　While thou art pouring forth thy soul abroad
　　　　　　In such an ecstasy!
　　Still wouldst thou sing, and I have ears in vain—
　　　　To thy high requiem become a sod.

Thou wast not born for death, immortal Bird!
   No hungry generations tread thee down;
The voice I hear this passing night was heard
   In ancient days by emperor and clown:
Perhaps the self-same song that found a path
      Through the sad heart of Ruth, when, sick for home,
         She stood in tears amid the alien corn;
               The same that oft times hath
      Charmed magic casements, opening on the foam
         Of perilous seas, in faery lands forlorn.

Forlorn! the very word is like a bell
   To toll me back from thee to my sole self!
Adieu! the fancy cannot cheat so well
   As she is famed to do, deceiving elf.
Adieu! adieu! thy plaintive anthem fades
      Past the near meadows, over the still stream,
         Up the hill-side; and now 'tis buried deep
               In the next valley-glades:
      Was it a vision, or a waking dream?
         Fled is that music:—do I wake or sleep?

John Keats

The Road Not Taken

Two roads diverged in a yellow wood,
And sorry I could not travel both
And be one traveler, long I stood
And looked down one as far as I could
To where it bent in the undergrowth;

Then took the other, as just as fair,
And having perhaps the better claim,
Because it was grassy and wanted wear;
Though as for that, the passing there
Had worn them really about the same,

And both that morning equally lay
In leaves no step had trodden black.
Oh, I kept the first for another day!
Yet knowing how way leads on to way,
I doubted if I should ever come back.

I shall be telling this with a sigh
Somewhere ages and ages hence:
Two roads diverged in a wood, and I—
I took the one less traveled by,
And that has made all the difference.

Robert Frost

Sympathy

I know what the caged bird feels, alas!
When the sun is bright on the upland slopes;
When the wind stirs soft through the springing grass
And the river flows like a stream of glass;
When the first bird sings and the first bud opes,
And the faint perfume from its chalice steals—
I know what the caged bird feels!

I know why the caged bird beats his wing
Till its blood is red on the cruel bars;
For he must fly back to his perch and cling
When he fain would be on the bough a-swing;
And a pain still throbs in the old, old scars
And they pulse again with a keener sting—
I know why he beats his wing!

I know why the caged bird sings, ah me,
When his wing is bruised and his bosom sore,—
When he beats his bars and would be free;
It is not a carol of joy or glee,
But a prayer that he sends from his heart's deep core,
But a plea, that upward to Heaven he flings—
I know why the caged bird sings!

Paul Laurence Dunbar

Leisure

What is this life if, full of care,
We have no time to stand and stare.

No time to stand beneath the boughs
And stare as long as sheep or cows.

No time to see, when woods we pass,
Where squirrels hide their nuts in grass.

No time to see, in broad daylight,
Streams full of stars like skies at night.

No time to turn at Beauty's glance,
And watch her feet, how they can dance.

No time to wait till her mouth can
Enrich that smile her eyes began.

A poor life this if, full of care,
We have no time to stand and stare.

W. H. Davies

Heaven

Fish (fly-replete, in depth of June,
Dawdling away their wat'ry noon)
Ponder deep wisdom, dark or clear,
Each secret fishy hope or fear.
Fish say, they have their Stream and Pond;
But is there anything Beyond?
This life cannot be All, they swear,
For how unpleasant, if it were!
One may not doubt that, somehow, Good
Shall come of Water and of Mud;
And, sure, the reverent eye must see
A Purpose in Liquidity.
We darkly know, by Faith we cry,
The future is not Wholly Dry.
Mud unto mud!—Death eddies near—
Not here the appointed End, not here!
But somewhere, beyond Space and Time,
Is wetter water, slimier slime!

And there (they trust) there swimmeth One
Who swam ere rivers were begun,
Immense, of fishy form and mind,
Squamous, omnipotent, and kind;
And under that Almighty Fin,
The littlest fish may enter in.
Oh! never fly conceals a hook,
Fish say, in the Eternal Brook,
But more than mundane weeds are there,
And mud, celestially fair;
Fat caterpillars drift around,
And Paradisal grubs are found;
Unfading moths, immortal flies,
And the worm that never dies.
And in that Heaven of all their wish,
There shall be no more land, say fish.

Rupert Brooke

"There is no God"

There is no God, the wicked saith,
   And truly it's a blessing,
For what he might have done with us
   It's better only guessing.

There is no God, a youngster thinks,
   Or really, if there may be,
He surely didn't mean a man
   Always to be a baby.

There is no God, or if there is,
   The tradesman thinks, 'twere funny
If he should take it ill in me
   To make a little money.

Whether there be, the rich man says,
   It matters very little,
For I and mine, thank somebody,
   Are not in want of victual.

Some others also to themselves
   Who scarce so much as doubt it,
Think there is none, when they are well,
   And do not think about it.

But country folks who live beneath
   The shadow of the steeple,
The parson and the parson's wife,
   And mostly married people,

Youths green and happy in first love,
    So thankful for illusion,
And men caught out in what the world
    Calls guilt, in first confusion,

And almost every one when age,
    Disease or sorrows strike him,
Inclines to think there is a God,
    Or something very like him.

Arthur Hugh Clough

Eternity

He who binds to himself a joy
Does the wingèd life destroy;
But he who kisses the joy as it flies
Lives in eternity's sunrise.

William Blake

Magna Est Veritas

Here, in this little Bay,
Full of tumultuous life and great repose,
Where, twice a day,
The purposeless, glad ocean comes and goes,
Under high cliffs, and far from the huge town,
I sit me down.
For want of me the world's course will not fail;
When all its work is done, the lie shall rot;
The truth is great, and shall prevail,
When none cares whether it prevail or not.

Coventry Patmore

The Coming of Good Luck

So good luck came, and on my roof did light
Like noiseless snow, or as the dew of night:
Not all at once, but gently, as the trees
Are by the sunbeams tickled by degrees.

Robert Herrick

Autumn Fires

In the other gardens
    And all up the vale,
From the autumn bonfires
    See the smoke trail!

Pleasant summer over
    And all the summer flowers,
The red fire blazes,
    The grey smoke towers.

Sing a song of seasons!
    Something bright in all!
Flowers in the summer,
    Fires in the fall!

Robert Louis Stevenson

A Word

A word is dead
    When it is said,
Some say.
I say it just
Begins to live
    That day.

Emily Dickinson

Adlestrop

Yes, I remember Adlestrop—
The name, because one afternoon
Of heat the express-train drew up there
Unwontedly. It was late June.

The steam hissed. Someone cleared his throat.
No one left and no one came
On the bare platform. What I saw
Was Adlestrop—only the name

And willows, willow-herb, and grass,
And meadowsweet, and haycocks dry,
No whit less still and lonely fair
Than the high cloudlets in the sky.

And for that minute a blackbird sang
Close by, and round him, mistier,
Farther and farther, all the birds
Of Oxfordshire and Gloucestershire.

Edward Thomas

Stopping by Woods on a Snowy Evening

Whose woods these are I think I know.
His house is in the village though;
He will not see me stopping here
To watch his woods fill up with snow.

My little horse must think it queer
To stop without a farmhouse near
Between the woods and frozen lake
The darkest evening of the year.

He gives his harness bells a shake
To ask if there is some mistake.
The only other sound's the sweep
Of easy wind and downy flake.

The woods are lovely, dark and deep,
But I have promises to keep,
And miles to go before I sleep,
And miles to go before I sleep.

Robert Frost

A Clear Midnight

This is thy hour O Soul, thy free flight into the wordless,
Away from books, away from art, the day erased,
   the lesson done,
Thee fully forth emerging, silent, gazing, pondering the
   themes thou lovest best,
Night, sleep, death and the stars.

Walt Whitman

An Epilogue

I have seen flowers come in stony places
And kind things done by men with ugly faces,
And the gold cup won by the worst horse at the races,
So I trust, too.

John Masefield

OF ANIMALS AND NATURE

Weathers

This is the weather the cuckoo likes,
    And so do I;
When showers betumble the chestnut spikes,
    And nestlings fly:
And the little brown nightingale bills his best,
And they sit outside at "The Travellers' Rest",
And maids come forth sprig-muslin drest,
And citizens dream of the south and west,
    And so do I.

This is the weather the shepherd shuns,
    And so do I;
When beeches drip in browns and duns,
    And thresh, and ply;
And hill-hid tides throb, throe on throe,
And meadow rivulets overflow,
And drops on gate-bars hang in a row,
And rooks in families homeward go,
    And so do I.

Thomas Hardy

Pied Beauty

Glory be to God for dappled things—
    For skies of couple-colour as a brinded cow;
       For rose-moles all in stipple upon trout that swim;
Fresh-firecoal chestnut-falls; finches' wings;
    Landscape plotted and pieced—fold, fallow, and plough;
       And áll trádes, their gear and tackle and trim.

All things counter, original, spare, strange;
    Whatever is fickle, freckled (who knows how?)
       With swift, slow; sweet, sour; adazzle, dim;
He fathers-forth whose beauty is past change:
                                Praise him.

Gerard Manley Hopkins

Autumn

A touch of cold in the Autumn night—
I walked abroad,
And saw the ruddy moon lean over a hedge
Like a red-faced farmer.
I did not stop to speak, but nodded,
And round about were the wistful stars
With white faces like town children.

T. E. Hulme

To Autumn

Season of mists and mellow fruitfulness!
   Close bosom-friend of the maturing sun;
Conspiring with him how to load and bless
   With fruit the vines that round the thatch-eaves run;
To bend with apples the mossed cottage-trees,
   And fill all fruit with ripeness to the core;
     To swell the gourd, and plump the hazel shells
With a sweet kernel; to set budding more,
   And still more, later flowers for the bees,
   Until they think warm days will never cease,
     For Summer has o'erbrimmed their clammy cells.

Who hath not seen thee oft amid thy store?
   Sometimes whoever seeks abroad may find
Thee sitting careless on a granary floor,
   Thy hair soft-lifted by the winnowing wind,
Or on a half-reaped furrow sound asleep,
   Drowsed with the fume of poppies, while thy hook
     Spares the next swath and all its twinèd flowers;
And sometimes like a gleaner thou dost keep
   Steady thy laden head across a brook;
   Or by a cider-press, with patient look,
     Thou watchest the last oozings hours by hours.

Where are the songs of Spring? Ay, where are they?
   Think not of them, thou hast thy music too,—
While barred clouds bloom the soft-dying day,
   And touch the stubble-plains with rosy hue;
Then in a wailful choir the small gnats mourn
   Among the river sallows, borne aloft
     Or sinking as the light wind lives or dies;
And full-grown lambs loud bleat from hilly bourn;
   Hedge-crickets sing; and now with treble soft
   The redbreast whistles from a garden-croft;
     And gathering swallows twitter in the skies.

John Keats

173

Thaw

Over the land freckled with snow half-thawed
The speculating rooks at their nests cawed
And saw from elm-tops, delicate as flower of grass,
What we below could not see, Winter pass.

Edward Thomas

In the Fields

Lord, when I look at lovely things which pass,
   Under old trees the shadows of young leaves
Dancing to please the wind along the grass,
   Or the gold stillness of the August sun
     on the August sheaves;
Can I believe there is a heavenlier world than this?
   And if there is
Will the strange heart of any everlasting thing
   Bring me these dreams that take my breath away?
They come at evening with the home-flying rooks
    and the scent of hay,
   Over the fields. They come in Spring.

. Charlotte Mew

Daffodils

I wandered lonely as a cloud
   That floats on high o'er vales and hills,
When all at once I saw a crowd,
   A host, of golden daffodils;
Beside the lake, beneath the trees,
Fluttering and dancing in the breeze.

Continuous as the stars that shine
   And twinkle on the Milky Way,
They stretched in never-ending line
   Along the margin of a bay:
Ten thousand saw I at a glance,
Tossing their heads in sprightly dance.

The waves beside them danced, but they
   Out-did the sparkling waves in glee:
A poet could not but be gay,
   In such a jocund company:
I gazed—and gazed—but little thought
What wealth the show to me had brought:

For oft, when on my couch I lie
   In vacant or in pensive mood,
They flash upon that inward eye
   Which is the bliss of solitude;
And then my heart with pleasure fills,
And dances with the daffodils.

William Wordsworth

"Loveliest of trees, the cherry now"

Loveliest of trees, the cherry now
Is hung with bloom along the bough,
And stands about the woodland ride
Wearing white for Eastertide.

Now, of my threescore years and ten,
Twenty will not come again,
And take from seventy springs a score,
It only leaves me fifty more.

And since to look at things in bloom
Fifty springs are little room,
About the woodlands I will go
To see the cherry hung with snow.

A. E. Housman

"Repeat that, repeat"

Repeat that, repeat,
Cuckoo, bird, and open ear wells, heart-springs,
   delightfully sweet,
With a ballad, with a ballad, a rebound
Off trundled timber and scoops of the hillside ground,
   hollow hollow hollow ground:
The whole landscape flashes on a sudden at a sound.

Gerard Manley Hopkins

All Things Bright and Beautiful

All things bright and beautiful,
All creatures great and small,
All things wise and wonderful,
The Lord God made them all.

Each little flower that opens,
Each little bird that sings,
He made their glowing colours,
He made their tiny wings:

The purple-headed mountain,
The river running by,
The sunset and the morning,
That brightens up the sky:

The cold wind in the winter,
The pleasant summer sun,
The ripe fruits in the garden,
He made them every one:

The tall trees in the greenwood,
The meadows for our play,
The rushes by the water
To gather every day:

He gave us eyes to see them,
And lips that we might tell
How great is God Almighty,
Who has made all things well.

Cecil Frances Alexander

"My heart leaps up"

My heart leaps up when I behold
   A rainbow in the sky:
So was it when my life began;
So is it now I am a man;
So be it when I shall grow old,
   Or let me die!
The Child is father of the Man;
And I could wish my days to be
Bound each to each by natural piety.

William Wordsworth

Triolet

"The child is father to the man."
How can he be? The words are wild.
Suck any sense from that who can:
"The child is father to the man."
No; what the poet did write ran,
"The man is father to the child."
"The child is father to the man"!
How *can* he be? The words are wild.

Gerard Manley Hopkins

The Lake Isle of Innisfree

I will arise and go now, and go to Innisfree,
And a small cabin build there, of clay and wattles made:
Nine bean-rows will I have there, a hive for the honey-bee,
And live alone in the bee-loud glade.

And I shall have some peace there, for peace comes
    dropping slow,
Dropping from the veils of the morning to where
    the cricket sings;
There midnight's all a glimmer, and noon a purple glow,
And evening full of the linnet's wings.

I will arise and go now, for always night and day
I hear lake water lapping with low sounds by the shore;
While I stand on the roadway, or on the pavements grey,
I hear it in the deep heart's core.

William Butler Yeats

Inversnaid

This darksome burn, horseback brown,
His rollrock highroad roaring down,
In coop and in comb the fleece of his foam
Flutes and low to the lake falls home.

A windpuff-bonnet of fáwn-fróth
Turns and twindles over the broth
Of a pool so pitchblack, féll-frówning,
It rounds and rounds Despair to drowning.

Degged with dew, dappled with dew
Are the groins of the braes that the brook treads through,
Wiry heathpacks, flitches of fern,
And the beadbonny ash that sits over the burn.

What would the world be, once bereft
Of wet and of wildness? Let them be left,
O let them be left, wildness and wet;
Long live the weeds and the wilderness yet.

Gerard Manley Hopkins

180

The Animals

They do not live in the world,
Are not in time and space.
From birth to death hurled
No word do they have, not one
To plant a foot upon,
Were never in any place.

For with names the world was called
Out of the empty air,
With names was built and walled,
Line and circle and square,
Dust and emerald;
Snatched from deceiving death
By the articulate breath.

But these have never trod
Twice the familiar track,
Never never turned back
Into the memoried day.
All is new and near
In the unchanging Here
Of the fifth great day of God,
That shall remain the same,
Never shall pass away.

On the sixth day we came.

Edwin Muir

The Tyger

Tyger! Tyger! burning bright
In the forests of the night,
What immortal hand or eye
Could frame thy fearful symmetry?

In what distant deeps or skies
Burned the fire of thine eyes?
On what wings dare he aspire?
What the hand dare seize the fire?

And what shoulder, and what art,
Could twist the sinews of thy heart?
And when thy heart began to beat,
What dread hand? And what dread feet?

What the hammer? What the chain?
In what furnace was thy brain?
What the anvil? What dread grasp
Dare its deadly terrors clasp?

When the stars threw down their spears,
And watered heaven with their tears,
Did he smile his work to see?
Did he who made the Lamb make thee?

Tyger! Tyger! burning bright
In the forests of the night,
What immortal hand or eye
Dare frame thy fearful symmetry?

William Blake

The Fallow Deer at the Lonely House

One without looks in to-night
    Through the curtain-chink
From the sheet of glistening white;
One without looks in to-night
    As we sit and think
    By the fender-brink.

We do not discern those eyes
    Watching in the snow;
Lit by lamps of rosy dyes
We do not discern those eyes
    Wondering, aglow,
    Fourfooted, tiptoe.

Thomas Hardy

The Yak

For hours the princess would not play or sleep
    Or take the air;
Her red mouth wore a look it meant to keep
    Unmelted there;
(Each tired courtier longed to shriek, or weep,
    But did not dare.)

Then one young duchess said: "I'll to the King,
    And short and flat
I'll say, 'Her Highness will not play or sing
    Or pet the cat;
Or feed the peacocks, or do anything—
    And that is that.' "

So to the King she went, curtsied, and said,
    (No whit confused):
"Your Majesty, I would go home! The court is dead.
    Have me excused;
The little princess still declines,"—she tossed her head—
    "To be amused."

Then to the princess stalked the King: "What ho!" he roared,
    "What may you lack?
Why do you look, my love, so dull and bored
    With all this pack
Of minions?" She answered, while he waved his sword:
    "I want a yak."

"A yak!" he cried (each courtier cried, "Yak! Yak!"
    As at a blow)
"Is that a figure on the zodiac?

Or horse? Or crow?"
The princess sadly said to him: "Alack
  I do not know."

"We'll send the vassals far and wide, my dear!"
  Then quoth the King:
"They'll make a hunt for it, then come back here
  And bring the thing,—
But warily,—lest it be wild, or queer,
  Or have a sting."

So off the vassals went, and well they sought
  On every track,
Till by and by in old Tibet they bought
  An ancient yak.
Yet when the princess saw it, she said naught
  But: "Take it back!"

And what the courtiers thought they did not say
  (Save soft and low).
For that is surely far the wisest way
  As we all know;
While for the princess? She went back to play!
                    Tra-rill-a-la-lo!
                    Tra-rill-a-la-lo!
                    Tra-rill-a-la-lo!

Virna Sheard

The Yak

As a friend to the children commend me the Yak,
   You will find it exactly the thing:
It will carry and fetch, you can ride on its back,
   Or lead it about with a string.

The Tartar who dwells on the plains of Thibet
   (A desolate region of snow)
Has for centuries made it a nursery pet,
   And surely the Tartar should know!

Then tell your papa where the Yak can be got,
   And if he is awfully rich
He will buy you the creature—or else he will *not*.
   (I cannot be positive which.)

Hilaire Belloc

Little Fish

The tiny fish enjoy themselves
in the sea.
Quick little splinters of life,
their little lives are fun to them
in the sea.

D. H. Lawrence

The Common Cormorant

The common cormorant or shag
Lays eggs inside a paper bag
The reason you will see no doubt
It is to keep the lightning out.
But what these unobservant birds
Have never noticed is that herds
Of wandering bears may come with buns
And steal the bags to hold the crumbs.

Christopher Isherwood

The Frog

What a wonderful bird the frog are!
When he stand he sit almost;
When he hop he fly almost.
He ain't got no sense hardly;
He ain't got no tail hardly either.
When he sit, he sit on what he ain't got almost.

Anon.

The Snare

I hear a sudden cry of pain!
There is a rabbit in a snare:
Now I hear the cry again,
But I cannot tell from where.

But I cannot tell from where
He is calling out for aid!
Crying on the frightened air,
Making everything afraid!

Making everything afraid!
Wrinkling up his little face!
As he cries again for aid;
—And I cannot find the place!

And I cannot find the place
Where his paw is in the snare!
Little One! Oh, Little One!
I am searching everywhere!

James Stephens

The Bells of Heaven

'Twould ring the bells of Heaven
The wildest peal for years,
If Parson lost his senses
And people came to theirs,
And he and they together
Knelt down with angry prayers
For tamed and shabby tigers
And dancing dogs and bears,
And wretched, blind pit ponies,
And little hunted hares.

Ralph Hodgson

The Eagle

He clasps the crag with crooked hands;
Close to the sun in lonely lands,
Ringed with the azure world, he stands.

The wrinkled sea beneath him crawls;
He watches from his mountain walls,
And like a thunderbolt he falls.

Alfred, Lord Tennyson

The Thought-Fox

I imagine this midnight moment's forest:
Something else is alive
Beside the clock's loneliness
And this blank page where my fingers move.

Through the window I see no star:
Something more near
Though deeper within darkness
Is entering the loneliness:

Cold, delicately as the dark snow
A fox's nose touches twig, leaf;
Two eyes serve a movement, that now
And again now, and now, and now

Sets neat prints into the snow
Between trees, and warily a lame
Shadow lags by stump and in hollow
Of a body that is bold to come

Across clearings, an eye,
A widening deepening greenness,
Brilliantly, concentratedly,
Coming about its own business

Till, with a sudden sharp hot stink of fox
It enters the dark hole of the head.
The window is starless still; the clock ticks,
The page is printed.

Ted Hughes

OF MAGIC AND MYSTERY

Dreams

Here we are all, by day; by night we are hurled
By dreams, each one into a several world.

Robert Herrick

Song: "Where the bee sucks, there suck I"

Where the bee sucks, there suck I,
  In a cowslip's bell I lie,
There I couch when owls do cry,
On the bat's back I do fly
After summer merrily.
Merrily, merrily, shall I live now
Under the blossom that hangs on the bough.

William Shakespeare

Eldorado

Gaily bedight,
A gallant knight,
In sunshine and in shadow,
Had journeyed long,
Singing a song,
In search of Eldorado.

But he grew old—
This knight so bold—
And o'er his heart a shadow
Fell as he found
No spot of ground
That looked like Eldorado.

And, as his strength
Failed him at length,
He met a pilgrim shadow:
"Shadow," said he,
"Where can it be,
This land of Eldorado?"

"Over the mountains
Of the Moon,
Down the valley of the Shadow,
Ride, boldly ride,"
The shade replied,
"If you seek for Eldorado."

Edgar Allan Poe

Romance

When I was but thirteen or so
   I went into a golden land,
Chimborazo, Cotopaxi
   Took me by the hand.

My father died, my brother too,
   They passed like fleeting dreams.
I stood where Popocatapetl
   In the sunlight gleams.

I dimly heard the Master's voice
   And boys far-off at play,
Chimborazo, Cotopaxi
   Had stolen me away.

I walked in a great golden dream
   To and fro from school—
Shining Popocatapetl
   The dusty streets did rule.

I walked home with a gold dark boy
   And never a word I'd say,
Chimborazo, Cotopaxi
   Had taken my speech away:

I gazed entranced upon his face
   Fairer than any flower—
O shining Popocatapetl
   It was thy magic hour:

The houses, people, traffic seemed
   Thin fading dreams by day,
Chimborazo, Cotopaxi
   They had stolen my soul away!

W. J. Turner

Jabberwocky

'Twas brillig, and the slithy toves
   Did gyre and gimble in the wabe:
All mimsy were the borogoves,
     And the mome raths outgrabe.

"Beware the Jabberwock, my son!
   The jaws that bite, the claws that catch!
Beware the Jubjub bird, and shun
     The frumious Bandersnatch!"

He took his vorpal sword in hand:
   Long time the manxome foe he sought—
So rested he by the Tumtum tree,
     And stood awhile in thought.

And, as in uffish thought he stood,
   The Jabberwock, with eyes of flame,
Came whiffling through the tulgey wood,
     And burbled as it came!

One, two! One, two! And through and through
   The vorpal blade went snicker-snack!
He left it dead, and with its head
     He went galumphing back.

"And hast thou slain the Jabberwock?
   Come to my arms, my beamish boy!
O frabjous day! Callooh! Callay!"
     He chortled in his joy.

'Twas brillig, and the slithy toves
   Did gyre and gimble in the wabe:
All mimsy were the borogoves,
     And the mome raths outgrabe.

Lewis Carroll

The Owl and the Pussy-cat

The Owl and the Pussy-cat went to sea
   In a beautiful pea-green boat,
They took some honey, and plenty of money,
   Wrapped up in a five-pound note.
The Owl looked up to the stars above,
   And sang to a small guitar,
"O lovely Pussy! O Pussy, my love,
   What a beautiful Pussy you are,
      You are,
      You are!
   What a beautiful Pussy you are!"

Pussy said to the Owl, "You elegant fowl!
   How charmingly sweet you sing!
O let us be married! too long we have tarried:
   But what shall we do for a ring?"
They sailed away for a year and a day,
   To the land where the Bong-tree grows,
And there in a wood a Piggy-wig stood,
   With a ring at the end of his nose,
      His nose,
      His nose,
   With a ring at the end of his nose.

"Dear Pig, are you willing to sell for one shilling
    Your ring?" Said the Piggy, "I will."
So they took it away, and were married next day
    By the Turkey who lives on the hill.
They dined on mince, and slices of quince,
    Which they ate with a runcible spoon;
And hand in hand, on the edge of the sand,
    They danced by the light of the moon,
        The moon,
        The moon,
    They danced by the light of the moon.

Edward Lear

Kubla Khan

In Xanadu did Kubla Khan
    A stately pleasure-dome decree:
Where Alph, the sacred river, ran
Through caverns measureless to man
    Down to a sunless sea.
So twice five miles of fertile ground
With walls and towers were girdled round:
And there were gardens bright with sinuous rills
Where blossomed many an incense-bearing tree;
And here were forests ancient as the hills,
Enfolding sunny spots of greenery.

But O, that deep romantic chasm which slanted
Down the green hill athwart a cedarn cover!
A savage place! as holy and enchanted
As e'er beneath a waning moon was haunted
By woman wailing for her demon-lover!
And from this chasm, with ceaseless turmoil seething,
As if this earth in fast thick pants were breathing,
A mighty fountain momently was forced;
Amid whose swift half-intermitted burst
Huge fragments vaulted like rebounding hail,
Or chaffy grain beneath the thresher's flail:
And 'mid these dancing rocks at once and ever
It flung up momently the sacred river.
Five miles meandering with a mazy motion
Through wood and dale the sacred river ran,
Then reached the caverns measureless to man,
And sank in tumult to a lifeless ocean:
And 'mid this tumult Kubla heard from far
Ancestral voices prophesying war!

The shadow of the dome of pleasure
Floated midway on the waves;
Where was heard the mingled measure
From the fountain and the caves.
It was a miracle of rare device,
A sunny pleasure-dome with caves of ice!

A damsel with a dulcimer
In a vision once I saw:
It was an Abyssinian maid,
And on her dulcimer she played,
Singing of Mount Abora.
Could I revive within me,
Her symphony and song,
To such a deep delight 'twould win me,
That with music loud and long,
I would build that dome in air,
That sunny dome! those caves of ice!
And all who heard should see them there,
And all should cry, Beware! Beware!
His flashing eyes, his floating hair!
Weave a circle round him thrice,
And close your eyes with holy dread,
For he on honey-dew hath fed,
And drunk the milk of Paradise.

Samuel Taylor Coleridge

The Song of Wandering Aengus

I went out to the hazel wood,
Because a fire was in my head,
And cut and peeled a hazel wand,
And hooked a berry to a thread;
And when white moths were on the wing,
And moth-like stars were flickering out,
I dropped the berry in a stream
And caught a little silver trout.

When I had laid it on the floor
I went to blow the fire aflame,
But something rustled on the floor,
And some one called me by my name:
It had become a glimmering girl
With apple blossom in her hair
Who called me by my name and ran
And faded through the brightening air.

Though I am old with wandering
Through hollow lands and hilly lands,
I will find out where she has gone,
And kiss her lips and take her hands;
And walk among long dappled grass,
And pluck till time and times are done
The silver apples of the moon,
The golden apples of the sun.

W. B. Yeats

Tom o' Bedlam

The moon's my constant mistress,
　　And the lovely owl my marrow;
　　　　The flaming drake,
　　　　And the night-crow, make
　　Me music to my sorrow.

I know more than Apollo;
　　For oft, when he lies sleeping,
　　　　I behold the stars
　　　　At mortal wars,
　　And the rounded welkin weeping.

The moon embraces her shepherd,
　　And the Queen of Love her warrior;
　　　　While the first does horn
　　　　The stars of the morn,
　　And the next the heavenly farrier.

With a heart of furious fancies,
　　Whereof I am commander:
　　　　With a burning spear,
　　　　And a horse of air,
　　To the wilderness I wander;

With a Knight of ghosts and shadows,
　　I summoned am to Tourney:
　　　　Ten leagues beyond
　　　　The wide world's end;
　　Methinks it is no journey.

　　　　　　Anon.

Spellbound

The night is darkening round me,
The wild winds coldly blow;
But a tyrant spell has bound me
And I cannot, cannot go.

The giant trees are bending
Their bare boughs weighed with snow.
And the storm is fast descending,
And yet I cannot go.

Clouds beyond clouds above me,
Wastes beyond wastes below;
But nothing drear can move me;
I will not, cannot go.

Emily Brontë

The Way Through the Woods

They shut the road through the woods
Seventy years ago.
Weather and rain have undone it again,
And now you would never know
There was once a road through the woods
Before they planted the trees.
It is underneath the coppice and heath
And the thin anemones.
Only the keeper sees
That, where the ring-dove broods,
And the badgers roll at ease,
There was once a road through the woods.

Yet, if you enter the woods
Of a summer evening late,
When the night-air cools on the trout-ringed pools
Where the otter whistles his mate,
(They fear not men in the woods,
Because they see so few)
You will hear the beat of a horse's feet,
And the swish of a skirt in the dew,
Steadily cantering through
The misty solitudes,
As though they perfectly knew
The old lost road through the woods . . .
But there is no road through the woods.

Rudyard Kipling

"Her strong enchantments failing"

Her strong enchantments failing,
    Her towers of fear in wreck,
Her limbecks dried of poisons
    And the knife at her neck,

The Queen of air and darkness
    Begins to shrill and cry,
"O young man, O my slayer,
    To-morrow you shall die."

O Queen of air and darkness,
    I think 'tis truth you say,
And I shall die to-morrow;
    But you will die to-day.

A. E. Housman

The Star

Twinkle, twinkle, little star,
How I wonder what you are!
Up above the world so high,
Like a diamond in the sky.

When the blazing sun is gone,
When he nothing shines upon,
Then you show your little light,
Twinkle, twinkle, all the night.

Then the traveller in the dark,
Thanks you for your tiny spark,
He could not see which way to go,
If you did not twinkle so.

In the dark blue sky you keep,
And often through my curtains peep,
For you never shut your eye,
Till the sun is in the sky.

As your bright and tiny spark,
Lights the traveller in the dark—
Though I know not what you are,
Twinkle, twinkle, little star.

Jane Taylor

La Belle Dame Sans Merci

"O what can ail thee, knight-at-arms,
  Alone and palely loitering?
The sedge has withered from the lake,
  And no birds sing.

"O what can ail thee, knight-at-arms,
  So haggard and so woe-begone?
The squirrel's granary is full,
  And the harvest's done.

"I see a lily on thy brow
  With anguish moist and fever dew;
And on thy cheek a fading rose
  Fast withereth too."

"I met a lady in the meads,
  Full beautiful—a faery's child,
Her hair was long, her foot was light,
  And her eyes were wild.

"I made a garland for her head,
  And bracelets too, and fragrant zone;
She looked at me as she did love,
  And made sweet moan.

"I set her on my pacing steed
  And nothing else saw all day long,
For sideways would she lean, and sing
  A faery's song.

"She found me roots of relish sweet,
    And honey wild and manna dew,
And sure in language strange she said,
        'I love thee true!'

"She took me to her elfin grot,
    And there she wept and sighed full sore;
And there I shut her wild, wild eyes
        With kisses four.

"And there she lullèd me asleep,
    And there I dreamed—Ah! woe betide!
The latest dream I ever dreamed
        On the cold hill's side.

"I saw pale kings and princes too,
    Pale warriors, death-pale were they all;
Who cried—'La belle Dame sans Merci
        Hath thee in thrall!'

"I saw their starved lips in the gloam
    With horrid warning gapèd wide,
And I awoke and found me here
        On the cold hill's side.

"And this is why I sojourn here
    Alone and palely loitering,
Though the sedge is withered from the lake,
        And no birds sing."

John Keats

Song: "Go and catch a falling star"

Go and catch a falling star,
   Get with child a mandrake root,
Tell me where all past years are,
   Or who cleft the Devil's foot;
Teach me to hear mermaids singing,
Or to keep off envy's stinging,
       And find
       What wind
Serves to advance an honest mind.

If thou beest born to strange sights,
   Things invisible to see,
Ride ten thousand days and nights
   Till Age snow white hairs on thee;
Thou, when thou return'st, wilt tell me
All strange wonders that befell thee,
       And swear
       No where
Lives a woman true and fair.

If thou find'st one, let me know;
   Such a pilgrimage were sweet.
Yet do not; I would not go,
   Though at next door we might meet.
Though she were true when you met her,
And last till you write your letter,
       Yet she
       Will be
False, ere I come, to two or three.

John Donne

"Stars, I have seen them fall"

Stars, I have seen them fall,
　　But when they drop and die
No star is lost at all
　　From all the star-sown sky.
The toil of all that be
　　Helps not the primal fault;
It rains into the sea,
　　And still the sea is salt.

A. E. Housman

The Night Has a Thousand Eyes

The night has a thousand eyes,
　　And the day but one;
Yet the light of the bright world dies
　　With the dying sun.

The mind has a thousand eyes,
　　And the heart but one;
Yet the light of a whole life dies
　　When love is gone.

Francis William Bourdillon

The Donkey

When fishes flew and forests walked
    And figs grew upon thorn,
Some moment when the moon was blood
    Then surely I was born.

With monstrous head and sickening cry
    And ears like errant wings,
The devil's walking parody
    On all four-footed things.

The tattered outlaw of the earth,
    Of ancient crooked will;
Starve, scourge, deride me: I am dumb,
    I keep my secret still.

Fools! For I also had my hour;
    One far fierce hour and sweet:
There was a shout about my ears,
    And palms before my feet.

G. K. Chesterton

I Saw a Stable

I saw a stable, low and very bare,
    A little child in the manger.
The oxen knew Him, had Him in their care,
    To men He was a stranger.
The safety of the world was lying there,
    And the world's danger.

Mary Coleridge

A Baby-Sermon

The lightning and thunder
    They go and they come;
But the stars and the stillness
    Are always at home.

George MacDonald

Journey of the Magi

"A cold coming we had of it,
Just the worst time of the year
For a journey, and such a long journey:
The ways deep and the weather sharp,
The very dead of winter."
And the camels galled, sore-footed, refractory,
Lying down in the melting snow.
There were times we regretted
The summer palaces on slopes, the terraces,
And the silken girls bringing sherbet.
Then the camel men cursing and grumbling
And running away, and wanting their liquor and women,
And the night-fires going out, and the lack of shelters,
And the cities hostile and the towns unfriendly
And the villages dirty and charging high prices:
A hard time we had of it.
At the end we preferred to travel all night,
Sleeping in snatches,
With the voices singing in our ears, saying
That this was all folly.

Then at dawn we came down to a temperate valley,
Wet, below the snow line, smelling of vegetation,
With a running stream and a water-mill beating the darkness,
And three trees on the low sky.
And an old white horse galloped away in the meadow.
Then we came to a tavern with vine-leaves over the lintel,
Six hands at an open door dicing for pieces of silver,
And feet kicking the empty wine-skins.
But there was no information, so we continued
And arrived at evening, not a moment too soon
Finding the place; it was (you may say) satisfactory.

All this was a long time ago, I remember,
And I would do it again, but set down
This set down
This: were we led all that way for
Birth or Death? There was a Birth, certainly,
We had evidence and no doubt. I had seen birth and death,
But had thought they were different; this Birth was
Hard and bitter agony for us, like Death, our death.
We returned to our places, these Kingdoms,
But no longer at ease here, in the old dispensation,
With an alien people clutching their gods.
I should be glad of another death.

T. S. Eliot

Christmas Song

Above the weary waiting world,
Asleep in chill despair,
There breaks a sound of joyous bells
Upon the frosted air.
And o'er the humblest rooftree, lo,
A star is dancing on the snow.

What makes the yellow star to dance
Upon the brink of night?
What makes the breaking dawn to glow
So magically bright,—
And all the earth to be renewed
With infinite beatitude?

The singing bells, the throbbing star,
The sunbeams on the snow,
And the awakening heart that leaps
New ecstasy to know,—
They all are dancing in the morn
Because a little child is born.

Bliss Carman

The Oxen

Christmas Eve, and twelve of the clock.
   "Now they are all on their knees,"
An elder said as we sat in a flock
   By the embers in hearthside ease.

We pictured the meek mild creatures where
   They dwelt in their strawy pen,
Nor did it occur to one of us there
   To doubt they were kneeling then.

So fair a fancy few would weave
   In these years! Yet, I feel,
If someone said on Christmas Eve,
   "Come; see the oxen kneel,

"In the lonely barton by yonder coomb
   Our childhood used to know,"
I should go with him in the gloom,
   Hoping it might be so.

Thomas Hardy

INDEX OF POETS

INDEX OF TITLES AND FIRST LINES

Titles are in *italic*. When the title repeats in the first line, only the first line is given.

ACKNOWLEDGEMENTS

We are indebted to the copyright holders for permission to reproduce certain poems:

W. H. Auden: "Song: Stop All the Clocks" (Twelve Songs IX) from *Collected Poems*, Faber & Faber. Reprinted by permission of Faber & Faber.

Hilaire Belloc: "Lord Finchley", "The False Heart" and "The Yak" from *Complete Verse*. Reprinted by permission of PFD on behalf of the Estate of Hilaire Belloc. © The Estate of Hilaire Belloc.

Laurence Binyon: "For the Fallen (September 1914)" from *Collected Poems*. Reprinted by permission of The Society of Authors on behalf of the Laurence Binyon Estate.

Francis Brabazon: "Victoria Market" from *Early Poems*, Beacon Hill Publishing, 1953.

Charles Causley: "Eden Rock" from *Collected Poems*, Macmillan. Reprinted by permission of David Higham Associates.

G. K. Chesterton: "The Donkey" from *The Wild Knight*. Reprinted by permission of A. P. Watt on behalf of the Royal Literary Fund.

E. E. Cummings: "i like my body when it is with your body" and "who knows if the moon's a balloon" from *Complete Poems 1904-1962*, edited by George J. Firmage. Reprinted by permission of W. W. Norton and Co., Inc., copyright © 1920, 1976, 1991 by the Trustees for the E. E. Cummings Trust and George James Firmage.

W. H. Davies: "Leisure" from *Complete Poems*. Reprinted by permission of Dee & Griffin, Solicitors, on behalf of the Mrs. H. M. Davies Will Trust.

Emily Dickinson: "In this short Life". Reprinted by permission of the publishers and the Trustees of Amherst College from *The Poems of Emily Dickinson*, Ralph W. Franklin, ed., Cambridge, Mass.: The Belknap Press of Harvard University Press. Copyright © 1998 by the President and Fellows of Harvard College. Copyright © 1951, 1955, 1979 by the President and Fellows of Harvard College.

T. S. Eliot: "Macavity: The Mystery Cat" and "The Journey of the Magi" from *Collected Poems*, Faber & Faber. Reprinted by permission of Faber & Faber.

James Fenton: "In a Notebook" and "The Skip" from *The Memory of War and Children in Exile: Poems 1968-1983*. Reprinted by permission of PFD on behalf of James Fenton. © James Fenton 1982, 1983.

Robert Frost: "Stopping by Woods on a Snowy Evening" and "The Road Not Taken" from *The Poetry of Robert Frost* edited by Edward Connery Lathem, Jonathan Cape. Reprinted by permission of The Random House Group Ltd on behalf of the Estate of Robert Frost.

Denis Glover: "The Magpies" from *Selected Poems*. Reprinted by permission of the Granville Glover Family Trust.

Harry Graham: "Mr. Jones" from *Ruthless Rhymes for Heartless Homes*, Edward Arnold. First published 1899.

Robert Graves: "A Slice of Wedding Cake" and "She tells her love while half asleep" from *Collected Poems*. Reprinted by permission of Carcanet Press Ltd and of A. P. Watt Ltd on behalf of The Trustees of the Robert Graves Copyright Trust.

Ivor Gurney: "To His Love" from *The Collected Poems of Ivor Gurney* edited by P. J. Kavanagh, Oxford University Press. Reprinted by permission of P. J. Kavanagh on behalf of the Gurney Estate.

Kevin Hart: "The Last Day" from *Your Shadow*, Angus & Robertson, 1984. Reprinted by permission of HarperCollins Australia.

Seamus Heaney: "The Railway Children" from *Station Island*, Faber & Faber. Reprinted by permission of Faber & Faber.

Ralph Hodgson: "The Bells of Heaven" from *Collected Poems*, Macmillan, 1961.

A. E. Housman: "Her Strong Enchantments Failing", "Into My Heart an Air that Kills", "Loveliest of Trees, the Cherry Now" and "Stars I Have Seen Them Fall" from *Collected Poems*. Reprinted by permission of The Society of Authors as the literary representative of the Estate of A. E. Housman.

Langston Hughes: "Life Is Fine" from *Collected Poems* (Knopf, 1994), copyright © 1994 by the Estate of Langston Hughes, reprinted by permission of David Higham Associates and Alfred A. Knopf Inc.

Ted Hughes: "The Thought-Fox" from *The Hawk in the Rain*, Faber & Faber. Reprinted by permission of Faber & Faber.

Christopher Isherwood: "The Common Cormorant", copyright The Estate of Christopher Isherwood, reproduced by permission of Curtis Brown Ltd, London on behalf of the Executors of the Estate of Christopher Isherwood.

M. K. Joseph: "Girl, Boy, Flower, Bicycle" from *Inscription on a Paper Dart: Selected Poems 1945-1972*, AUP/OUP, 1974. Reprinted by permission of Mrs M. J. Joseph.

Patrick Kavanagh: "On Raglan Road". Reprinted by permission of Peter Kavanagh from *The Complete Poems of Patrick Kavanagh*, New York, 1996, edited and with commentary by Peter Kavanagh. Copyright 1972, 1996 Peter Kavanagh.

Rudyard Kipling: "Common Form", "If–", "There is pleasure in the wet, wet clay" and "The Way Through the Woods" from *The Definitive Edition of Rudyard Kipling's Verse*, Hodder and Stoughton. Reprinted by permission of A. P. Watt Ltd on behalf of The National Trust for Places of Historic Interest or Natural Beauty.

Philip Larkin: "Days" and "This Be The Verse" from *Collected Poems*, Faber & Faber. Reprinted by permission of Faber & Faber.

D. H. Lawrence: "Desire Is Dead", "Self-Pity" and "What Ails Thee?" from *The Complete Poems of D. H. Lawrence*, William Heinemann Ltd. Reprinted by permission of Lawrence Pollinger Ltd and the Estate of Frieda Lawrence Ravagli.

Louis MacNeice: "Apple Blossom" from *Collected Poems*, Faber & Faber. Reprinted by permission of David Higham Associates.

John Masefield: "An Epilogue", "Cargoes" and "Sea-Fever" from *Collected Poems*. Reprinted by permission of The Society of Authors as the literary representative of the Estate of John Masefield.

Edna St. Vincent Millay: "First Fig" and "The Unexplorer" from *Collected Poems*, HarperCollins. Copyright 1922, 1950 by Edna St. Vincent Millay. All rights reserved. Reprinted by permission of Elizabeth Barnett, literary executor.

A. A. Milne: "The King's Breakfast" from *When We Were Very Young*, © A. A. Milne. Copyright under the Berne Convention. Published by Methuen, an imprint of Egmont Children's Books Limited, London, and used with permission.

Adrian Mitchell: "Celia Celia" © Adrian Mitchell. Available in *Heart on the Left* 1997. Reprinted by permission of PFD on behalf of Adrian Mitchell. Educational Health Warning! Adrian Mitchell asks that none of his poems are used in connection with any examinations whatsoever.

Edwin Muir: "The Animals" from *The Collected Poems of Edwin Muir*, Faber & Faber. Reprinted by permission of Faber & Faber.

Ogden Nash: "Reflection on Ice-Breaking" from *Candy Is Dandy: The Best of Ogden Nash*, Methuen. Reprinted by permission of Methuen Publishing Ltd.

Dorothy Parker: "Résumé" from *The Portable Dorothy Parker*, copyright © 1926, 1928, 1931, 1954, 1956, 1959 by Dorothy Parker, Gerald Duckworth & Co.

Kathleen Raine: "Spell of Creation" from *Collected Poems*, Hamish Hamilton, 1981.

Virna Sheard: "The Yak" from *Leaves in the Wind*, 1938.

Stevie Smith: "Advice to Young Children" and "Not Waving, but Drowning" from *The Collected Poems* (Penguin 20th-Century Classics). Reprinted by permission of James MacGibbon.

James Stephens: "The Snare" from *Collected Poems*, Macmillan, 1954.

Dylan Thomas: "Do Not Go Gentle into that Good Night" from *Collected Poems*, J. M. Dent. Reprinted by permission of David Higham Associates.

R. S. Thomas: "Children's Song" from *Collected Poems: 1949-1990*, J. M. Dent. Reprinted by permission of The Orion Publishing Group Ltd.

W. J. Turner: "Romance" from *Selected Poems 1916-1936*, Oxford University Press, 1939. First printed in *The Hunter and Other Poems*, 1916.

Judith Wright: "To a Child" from *A Human Pattern: Selected Poems*, ETT Imprint, Sydney, 1996. Reprinted by permission of ETT Imprint.

William Carlos William: "This Is Just to Say" from *Collected Poems, vol. 1*, Carcanet. Reprinted by permission of Carcanet Press Ltd.

W. B. Yeats: "He Wishes for the Cloths of Heaven", "The Lake Isle of Innisfree" and "The Song of Wandering Aengus" from *Collected Poems*, Macmillan. Reprinted by permission of A. P. Watt Ltd on behalf of Michael B. Yeats.

Although every effort has been made to trace and contact copyright holders in time for publication, this has not been possible in all cases. If notified, we will be pleased to rectify any errors or omissions at the earliest opportunity.